Resumes That Will
Get You the Job You Want

Resumes That Will Get You the Job You Want

A N D R E A   K A Y

BETTERWAY BOOKS

CINCINNATI, OHIO

Resumes That Will Get You the Job You Want. Copyright © 1997
by Andrea G. Kay. Printed and bound in the United States of
America. All rights reserved. No part of this book may be
reproduced in any form or by any electronic or mechanical means
including information storage and retrieval systems without
permission in writing from the publisher, except by a reviewer, who
may quote brief passages in a review. Published by Betterway
Books, an imprint of F&W Publications, Inc., 1507 Dana Avenue,
Cincinnati, Ohio 45207. (800) 289-0963. First edition.

Other fine Betterway Books are available from your local bookstore
or direct from the publisher.

02 01 00 99 98   6 5 4 3 2

Library of Congress Cataloging-in-Publication Data

Kay, Andrea G.
    Resumes that will get you the job you want / Andrea G. Kay.
        p.   cm.
    Includes index.
    ISBN 1-55870-455-8 (alk. paper)
    1. Résumés (Employment) 2. Applications for positions. I. Title.
HF5383.K39 1997
808'.06665—dc21   97-4922
                                                        CIP

Edited by Joyce Dolan
Production Edited by Michelle Kramer
Interior designed by Brian Roeth
Cover designed by Kathleen DeZarn

ABOUT THE AUTHOR

Andrea Kay is a career consultant. Since 1988 she has written over 450 articles on careers and job hunting as writer of the weekly newspaper column "Ask Andrea." She is host of the radio talk show *Job Talk*, which she started in 1991. She also gives weekly career advice on an ABC Television affiliate. She wrote the book *Interview Strategies That Will Get You the Job You Want*.

She has counseled thousands of job hunters and presented hundreds of seminars on resumes and job-hunting strategies to people in all types of professions who work in Fortune 100 companies, small and nonprofit businesses.

With a background in communications and advertising, her finely honed skills help people package and position themselves in the marketplace.

She's been widely quoted and interviewed in publications that include *Mademoiselle, Redbook, Woman, First for Women, U.S. Air Magazine* and on radio stations across the U.S. and Canada. She also wrote and narrated the videotape *Common Mistakes in Interviews and How to Overcome Them*, published by Cambridge Educational.

Recognition includes the Women in Communications Gem Award for adherence to the highest standards of practice in professional communications, support of women in the workforce and being a friend to job seekers.

She is a sought-after keynote and workshop presenter, speaking to national professional groups who named her Outstanding Speaker and Program of the Year. She has also addressed state and federal legislators on the plight of white-collar workers.

Kay received her B.A. degree from Kent State University, and her continuing education includes coursework in Gestalt stress management, building self-esteem, use of self in psychotherapy, Spanish, painting and drawing. She lives in Cincinnati, Ohio.

ACKNOWLEDGMENTS

THANK YOU TO:

My clients, readers of my column and others who sent good and bad examples of resumes.

Peter Mark Roget, who in 1852 created the original version of my *Roget's International Thesaurus* that I've lugged around since junior high school.

John Birge, musician and classical music aficionado; Jeff Krys, all-around music aficionado; Michele Naylor, researcher extraordinaire; Dan Barth, overall knowlegeable human being.

The following professionals: Bill Radin, recruiter; Monica Weakley, human resource specialist; Lauren Niemes, Greater Cincinnati Dietetic Association; Jack Wright, electronic resume specialist; Bill Warren, online expert; Pam Dixon, author; Dennis Rutherford, desktop publishing expert; David Torchia, employment attorney; and Joyce Dolan, editor.

Special, special thanks to Joy Dill for her objectivity, professional opinion and time when she was trying to take a break. And to Greg, for reading every word—several times.

TABLE OF CONTENTS

There are no dull people, there are only dull resumes.

Ya Gotta Be You

When you were born, everyone oohed and aahed over your adorable little ears and hands and feet and the way you cooed when they tickled your chin. Every inch of you was utterly special.

Since then, the world has done everything in its power to get you to look and act exactly like everyone else. You've been brainwashed to fit in and look and think like the crowd.

Boooring. And that's probably what's wrong with your resume.

The way I see it, it's because of this brainwashing—that you should look and sound just like the next person—and some erroneous resume myths that have been passed down through generations, that you think your resume should fit a particular mold.

See if these sound familiar. You think a resume should be one page (heaven forbid, not more than two). You should list job titles exactly as they were on your job description (even if no one outside your company will have the slightest idea what you did). Your resume should fit the jobs "that are out there." You can't say *that* (whatever) on a resume! A resume should *always* (fill in the blank).

So when you sit down to create yours, you end up with a play-it-safe yawner. You have a page or two of gobbledygook of what you think a resume is

supposed to be, which makes you just another musty, average name on a page. A walking zombie. You sound like everybody else.

Ever noticed what sells most? Things that have moxie. The guts to be different from everything else. Take *Pulp Fiction*, a 1994 feature film that didn't fit into any marketable movie genre like romantic comedy, action adventure, drama or suspense. It has netted $176.8 million worldwide. Yet, talk to Hollywood producers and they'll tell you a movie needs to fit a specific formula to be a success.

In a 1994 interview, jazz musician Dave Brubeck said this about "Take Five," a piece of music his group wrote: "Columbia Records said that no one could dance to it. It was against everything they told their artists not to do. They said that it wouldn't sell. They tried to stop it." "Take Five" not only made the pop charts, but turned out to be the strongest jazz album ever recorded.

Another example of how different is good is the Beatles. On February 11, 1964, they were on their first tour in America. In its 1995 Beatle Reunion Special, *LIFE* quoted *The Washington Post* as describing them as "asexual and homely." But more than seven thousand fans jammed the coliseum in Washington to see for themselves. The Beatles were treated rudely during a British Embassy reception that same day. Someone walked up to Ringo and cut off a piece of his hair. When Prime Minister Sir Alec Douglas-Home arrived at the White House the next day for a meeting with President Lyndon B. Johnson, LBJ said, "I like your advance guard, but don't you think they need haircuts?"

Two weeks later, hundreds of teenage girls held a nonstop vigil outside New York City's Plaza Hotel where the Beatles were staying, chanting "She Loves You." Six months later they arrived in the U.S. for a tour that included twenty-six concerts in thirty-four days.

There are countless examples like these. Examples of what the world will tell you things are supposed to be, look and sound like. And then somebody does something with spunk, expresses ideas and concepts in a fresh way, and everybody loves it and proves this common wisdom wrong. Which goes to show that people are attracted to things that are different from all the rest. They are drawn to the unexpected.

This book is about how to create a marketing tool that engages, breaks the mold, creates an impression, shows how utterly special you are and gets employers to sit up and take notice of you. After all, isn't that what you want?

If so, your resume better not squeak along with the masses. It better have zing, be bold, conspicuous, notable and shout, "I'm one heck of a problem solver with skills galore, oozing with knowledge, boundless potential and a fantastic personality to boot."

You don't have to be a wonderful writer to create a resume like that. You do need guts to throw away your preconceived notions. And time to devote to this and this only, then really buckle down. You'll need to write out information that's not at your fingertips. You may have to dig around in some dusty files and in your memory of years gone by.

My book will show you how to write a resume with oomph. One that not only grabs attention, but holds it. You'll see why you don't need to fret about whether your resume is one or two pages. Whether you've got a two-year gap or no experience at all. Whether you're fifty-five or twenty-five.

Follow the steps in this book, and you'll create a resume that:

- Positions you for the job you want
- Builds on your past experience (or lack of it)

- Minimizes preconceptions employers might have about you and your background
- Delivers a personal message about who you are and what you can do
- Breaks through the clutter of all the other resumes
- Helps you get to know you and talk about yourself in interviews

You may not agree with everything I say. Or someone you know may not see eye to eye with my strategies. I offer you what has worked for others. You need to consider your particular circumstances. Weigh this information and use what works for *you*.

Your resume itself will not get you a job. You'll wind up doing that on your own. But you do need one to get considered for most jobs. You'll be running neck and neck with other candidates. So first, yours has to get read. The kind of resume I'll show you how to create will dramatically increase those odds. Then to be considered for a position, you have to give proof—in a flash—that you have what an employer is looking for. Your resume, if it's done right, will do exactly that.

The kind of resume you can create with the help of this book will not be perfect. There is no such thing. It will not say what you think employers want to hear. (Who knows what that is?) It will not be written to fit the jobs "out there." We're trying to get you the job *you* want, remember?

It will capture your individuality, experience, skills and key information, downplay potential liabilities and position you the way you want to be perceived. It will show an employer a potential fit. It will do what a resume is supposed to do (which most don't): hook and hold someone's attention and show her how you can improve her life.

HOW TO USE THIS BOOK

I've written it in order of the logical steps it takes to write this type of resume. So I hope you'll start with chapter one and read the chapters in order. But if you're a skipper, try to hold off until you get through chapter four.

Chapter one explains how your resume gets around, what to send with it, the four things everyone wants to see on your resume and the one and only thing to concentrate on to create a resume that positions you the way you want. It's the foundation for everything else I talk about. There's a simple but very important exercise in this chapter.

Chapter two draws out of you the relevant information that could go on your resume, from what you know and can do to what kind of person you are. You'll create the guts of your resume in chapter three with a technique for figuring out what goes on or gets left off. Don't miss this. It also helps you describe what you want in your next position and why someone would hire you.

In chapter four you'll organize the relevant information you wrote in chapter two. I explain various resume sections, what they tell employers and optional ways to categorize information. I also cover dumb things people include and don't need to.

You'll learn pointers on how to write snappy phrases, make complicated things sound simple and boring things sound interesting. Those tips are in chapter five.

Chapter six helps you maneuver, highlight or downplay information about your present circumstances or past—no matter how bad you think they are—which leads to fewer misunderstandings. In chapter seven you'll learn how to make your resume easy to read and inviting plus details, pros and cons on sending resumes electronically.

Resume samples are in chapter eight. They're organized by profession or a situation someone's in, as new graduate resumes and yechy resumes—examples of what not to do.

By the time you get to the end, you'll know how to create a marketing tool that separates you from the pack and shows employers how you can make life better. You'll be closer to getting the job you want because now you can show them what makes you so special.

chapter one

Resumes That Get Around

asically, I'm an optimistic person. But I'm also realistic. That's why we need to set the record straight right here and now about resumes and their role in the universe.

A resume is not a job-hunting technique. Unfortunately, that's how many people use their resume. They mail off hundreds of them, hoping that someone will have on opening. Or they spend all of their time mailing their resumes in response to ads. Eventually, these people become sorely disappointed and waste a lot of time, stamps, envelopes, paper and typewriter ribbon or computer printer cartridges. They begin to think there's something wrong with their resume—or worse, them—because they get zilch response.

Even if you have a terrific resume, if you're using it as a job-hunting technique, you're asking too much of it. Resumes are marketing tools. They get around and get action because you used them while implementing a proven job-hunting technique.

Sure you can get a job by answering an ad. It's also possible that one of the five hundred companies you sent your resume to did actually need someone at the precise moment your resume landed on someone's desk. But odds are slim. Even when you answer ads, you're competing with hundreds—possibly thousands—of other people who read the same ad.

I'm not suggesting you never answer an ad. Just don't make this your only approach. Your dreams will be dashed if you use your resume solely to speak on your behalf to people who don't know you.

In this chapter you'll see how resumes get around when used as marketing tools. I focus on how and when you use your resume, how your resume is viewed and what people do with it once they receive it.

I'm also going to show you—starting here—resume-writing techniques that helped make effective marketing tools for hundreds of people.

These people used various job-hunting techniques. Sometimes a resume was passed on to someone who knew someone who had an opening. Or someone was so intrigued by what he saw in the resume, he met the job hunter and eventually created a position for her. Other people sent their resumes in response to openings they heard about. Their resumes got them the first interviews for the job.

One more thing, if you have a resume that you wrote based on what a half dozen other people told you to say, do us both a favor and throw it away. At least hide it in a drawer for now and don't think about it. Most likely it's not the kind of resume that will command much attention.

Every man, woman and child has an opinion on

what you should list on your resume and how to say it. It is very nice of them to offer advice. But if you created a resume with input from all these different people, your resume will reflect it. It will be a hodge-podge of opinions instead of a drop-dead marketing tool.

To write that kind of resume, you have to accept a few things.

The Truth

- The business world is full of incredibly busy people.
- They don't care that you need or want a new job. They have their own problems.
- They are inundated with hundreds of bits of information a day from TV, radio, magazines and newspapers, not to mention billboards, e-mail, cellular phones, office memos and bumper stickers.
- They see things from the perspective of, What's in it for me? (Although they may not think it consciously.)

So you need a document that not only introduces you to these busy people, but *hooks and holds their attention and—in a blink—shows them you have the potential to improve their lives or the life of someone they know.*

This is what your resume does *if* it's doing its job.

Sure you can write something that just lists all your jobs and when you had them. You can even use a resume service that does it for you. One of my clients told me Sears has a service that writes your resume for $75. Sure enough, I found it listed in the phone book, right after Refrigerators. I could never get anyone to answer the phone, so I can't tell you anything more about it. However, I do have a tough time understanding how you'd get the kind of resume that really captures your individuality for $75.

But is a one-size-fits-all format or a resume that just lists your jobs going to get me to notice you when I've got fourteen other things on my mind? Or when it comes in the mail along with 105 other resumes? Or when I'm trying to fill a position with the perfect person? Will that get me excited enough to refer you to someone I know? I don't think so.

The kind of resume that can do that will:

- Capture the most unique and interesting facts and characteristics about you that support your immediate career goal
- Tell what skills and knowledge you have
- Give an overview of your career—what you've done and where
- Show how you've made things better in the past and what you have the potential of doing in the future
- Use attention-grabbing, specific, action-oriented language
- Invite someone to want to know more

That's my definition of the kind of resume that will get you to the first step of getting the job you want.

Everyone Expects One

If you're job hunting, you'll be holding all kinds of meetings, from job interviews to informational meetings (these are times you meet with people you know or people you get referred to to get information and advice about your career). You'll answer ads in trade journals and newspapers, respond to openings you hear about and meet people in all kinds of situations.

The first thing out of most people's mouths will be, "Give me a copy of your resume." (I'm not suggesting you necessarily give it to them. There's enough wasted paper in the world. We'll talk about this later.) Your resume will be something you either send to someone *before* they meet you or leave with them or send to them *after* you meet.

If you're applying for a position within your present company, you'll also need a resume.

You may be asked for a resume if you're being considered as a board member of an organization.

The fact is, if you're going to market yourself, everyone just expects one. The question is, *What are they looking for?*

Most Everyone Wants to Know Four Things:

- What can you do?
- Have you done it and stuck with it?
- What do you know?
- What kind of person are you?

The other question is, *Why do they want your resume and what will they do with it?* Let's look at our various resume collectors in the world and, in their words, what they look for and why.

RESUME COLLECTORS
Recruiters
WHY THEY WANT YOUR RESUME

They have positions to fill and think you might fit one of them. They're screening you to see if you have the experience, skills and potential their clients are looking for.

WHAT THEY LOOK FOR AND WHAT CLUES THEM IN

• *Job stability*

If you've had fifteen jobs in ten years, the recruiters will wonder what's going on.

They'll also look at your resume format. One recruiter told me he assumes someone is hiding something if the resume *only* summarizes experience as opposed to summarizing *and* listing dates and places worked.

One human resource professional who works closely with recruiters said recruiters sometimes use resumes to learn what technologies are utilized in certain companies, which can be proprietary information. In chapter four I discuss how to deal with this dilemma of presenting yourself effectively without jeopardizing confidentiality.

• *Career continuity*

They look for people who haven't changed careers a lot. If you've been in real estate for two years, shoe sales for one year, investment banking and landscaping, a red flag goes up.

• *Professionalism*

They're looking for typographical errors, grammar and, overall, whether your resume looks neat, well thought-out and professional.

• *Competency in key areas*

They want to see that you have particular skills and knowledge. For example, if the recruiter has a position in desktop publishing, he may look for experience in QuarkXPress. If he needs an operations manager for a retail store, he may look for skills in planning and training and expertise in vendor negotiations.

WHAT THEY WILL DO WITH IT

File it, put it in a database, throw it away if it has no value to them or send it to their clients, depending on their arrangement. A recruiter who specializes in a particular niche and gets ten to fifty unsolicited resumes a week told me he only keeps one or two a month.

A larger recruiting firm that handles many professionals is more apt to put your resume in a database.

Human Resource Professionals
WHY THEY WANT YOUR RESUME

There's an opening in the company and policy requires you send one to apply for the job. They want to screen you to see if you have the experience, skills and potential the job calls for and if it's worth their time to interview you.

WHAT THEY LOOK FOR AND WHAT CLUES THEM IN

• *Job stability*

They look at length of time. This may clue them in on your ability to stick to something. A senior human resource specialist at a bank who recruits for entry-level to upper-management positions says she likes to see someone at the same company for five to seven years. Others want to see three to five years.

• *Competency in key areas*

For example, if a company is looking for an assistant to the president, they'll want to know if you can handle confidential correspondence, plan and coordinate meetings and travel arrangements.

Sometimes qualifications will be more specific. For instance, they might want a definite number of years of experience, a particular background, a certain software experience or college major.

• *Gaps in work history*

They won't necessarily discount you for gaps, but if it's a pattern, it says something. And you'll probably be asked about it during interviews.

• *An objective that reflects the job (This is a statement that describes what you are looking for. Details in chapter three.)*

One human resource person told me she detests objectives that read, "A challenging position that will utilize my areas of expertise." So do I. Don't get me wrong. I'm not suggesting you write an objective that states an exact job title of each job you want. (We get into this later.) But don't say something as vague and meaningless as "A challenging position that will utilize my areas of expertise."

• *Professionalism*

Good grammar and no typographical errors. Poor grammar and spelling mistakes are a telltale sign you just whipped through your resume, said the same human resource person. Which will make her wonder, "Is that how you'll handle the job?"

WHAT THEY WILL DO WITH IT

Put it in a file, throw it away or pass it on to the person who will follow up with you. One human resource person says her company doesn't throw away *any* resumes. For legal reasons, they really do keep them on file for six months, then store them.

Other People in Companies

Anybody who works for a company can be your potential link to their organization. Even if they aren't the person who does the hiring, they can always pass your resume to the one who does. In smaller companies, the person who heads a department may be responsible for the hiring.

WHY THEY WANT YOUR RESUME

They may know of a definite or possible opening in the future and want to see who's available or begin interviewing.

WHAT THEY LOOK FOR AND WHAT CLUES THEM IN

In general, they'll look for things that are similar to those the human resource professional and recruiter look for: basic qualifications, skills, expertise, stability and professionalism.

Specifics will depend on the position, the company and the person. For instance, if it's a small company with an entrepreneurial spirit, they may want a versatile, highly creative person who can wear many hats. If it's a company that wants to grow, they probably want innovative thinkers and risk takers.

WHAT THEY WILL DO WITH IT

File it, pass it around the department or follow up with you.

Friends, Family and Other Well-Meaning Folks

WHY THEY WANT YOUR RESUME

They think they may be able to help you find a position or refer you to someone who can help you.

WHAT THEY LOOK FOR AND WHAT CLUES THEM IN

They too will look for the same things everyone else looks for: qualifications, skills, stability and professionalism. Basically, relatives want to know if you've had good, decent jobs and if they want to claim you as someone they're related to.

WHAT THEY WILL DO WITH IT

Give it to someone, file it or stick it in a drawer at home with the Scotch tape and extra set of keys.

Now That You've Met

Your resume takes on new meaning after employers see you in the flesh. When you walk out the door, they're only left with the resume. They can now compare what they saw in person with what they see on paper. They will use it to judge or verify what they perceived. Are you really as organized as you said you are in the interview by the way your resume is written? Do you present yourself the way you described in your resume?

What Can You Learn From This?

What I already mentioned, but it can't hurt to say again (you're going to hear this one a lot):

MOST EVERYONE WANTS TO KNOW FOUR THINGS:
- What can you do?
- Have you done it and stuck with it?
- What do you know?
- What kind of person are you?

HOW YOUR RESUME LOOKS AND IS WRITTEN GREATLY AFFECTS HOW YOU'RE PERCEIVED

You can claim to be detail oriented and have a track record as an accurate editor, but if your resume has errors, smudges or dog-eared corners, someone will be prone to believe what he sees in front of him.

If you use terms such as *etc.* instead of saying what you mean, you may come across as lazy.

YOU CAN'T PLEASE EVERYONE

Each person will have a different perspective. You can be sensitive to the kinds of things that most people will notice. You can anticipate what someone in a particular industry or with a certain viewpoint will look for. You can guess how the usage of a certain phrase, deletion of something else or a particular format might be perceived.

But if you're asking me, "What will 'they' think if you put such and such words on your resume or don't list something else?" I'd be lying if I said anything but, "Beats me." I could guess. But everyone is different. Everyone will have their own unique perspective (and prejudices).

One human resource person told me her company has a list of twenty-three reasons for finding someone incompatible or unsuitable for hiring. They may decide just from looking at your resume that you fall into one of those twenty-three categories. How in the world can you prepare for that?

So you can't create a resume that will satisfy everyone. Don't even try. You can only create a resume that satisfies you. One that is truthful, positions you the way you want and:

- Keeps in mind the four general things people look for
- Is written in concise, dynamic language without errors of any kind
- Hooks and holds someone's attention and shows them you have the potential to improve their life

Once you've done that, and assuming you're applying for positions you're qualified for, this increases your chances that the recruiter, human resource professional or other decision maker will get excited enough to want to talk with you.

NO ABSOLUTE RULES

Since there are no perfect resumes, there are not absolute rules for writing one either.

There are, however, some general formats you can consider and key information to include in yours. (Chapter four goes into detail on this.) But *you* get to pick and choose which format and information to use that lets you best market yourself.

See, that's the whole point of creating a resume that *positions you the way you want.*

For example, if I had a pair of blue suede shoes for sale and you were interested in buying them, here's what I'd want you to know:

- They look rich and luxurious.
- They're extremely comfortable.
- They really jazz up an otherwise plain outfit.

Not:

- They're a pain in the neck to care for.
- They get ruined in the rain.
- They only last a season or two.

Even though the last three points may be true, this information will not encourage you to want to buy them. So I'm not going to bring them up. I wouldn't deny them if *you* brought them up in conversation, but that's a whole other issue.

Apply this logic when you write your resume. When trying to decide what to include and how to say it, look for ways to enhance others' perceptions of you, not take away from it.

For example, if you just graduated with a degree in music and want to be in a performing group, you'd bring up information and evidence that demonstrate your ability and potential to do that job. That includes:

- Abilities—What can you do? Sing, act, dance, work well with others, handle rigorous rehearsal schedules, follow instructions.
- Related experiences—Have you done it and stuck with it? Choruses you sang in and plays you acted in or other experiences that demonstrate your ability to do what the job requires.
- Knowledge—What do you know? Music theory, stage direction, modern dance, ballet, jazz, foreign languages.
- Personal attributes—What kind of person are you? Self-disciplined, enthusiastic, dependable, passionate, tenacious, patient.

You cover the four general areas people want to know about. And you forget about information that doesn't support that.

You're not trying to fool anyone. You wouldn't lie about the fact that you have no paid experience as a dancer or singer, if that's the case. But you don't need to advertise it either.

There's only one rule I lay down the law on: Be

strategic. *Pick and choose information that supports your objective.* (I define your objective in great deal in chapter three.) Think through the best place to put that information so that it logically supports your objective. Be selective with the words you use.

If you cling to unnecessary rules, you can't be strategic. You're too busy trying to follow rules instead of creating a marketing tool.

Rigid Resume Syndrome

I should point out that there are people who don't see eye to eye with me. They will tell you there are absolute rules for writing resumes and are not shy about telling you what those are.

I call this Rigid Resume Syndrome (RRS). Never heard of it? It runs rampant among job hunters, professional resume writers and your average Joe.

RRS causes job hunters to lose sleep because they lie in bed at night worrying. It creates tense resume writers who pace the room trying to figure out how they'll come up with that statement the people with RRS told them they had to have. It creates premature baldness for resume writers who can't seem to come up with the exact right wording and pull their hair out in frustration.

Beware of people who, when talking about resumes, start sentences with, "A resume must always. . . ." They are probably afflicted with RRS.

WHEN AND HOW YOU USE YOUR RESUME
To Respond to Openings Listed in an Advertisement

Before you fold up your resume and stick it in an envelope, consider hand delivering it if the company is in town.

Call the person who requested the resume and say, "I'll be in the area. Would it be OK if I dropped off my resume?" If he's available, he could say, "Sure, and stop by when you come in." You can suggest this if he doesn't. If he doesn't want to meet, he'll say so. At least you get the chance to check out the place, and, possibly, he'll get to meet you. You're no longer a faceless name on a piece of paper. You're a live human. Your resume gets more inter-

est. Even if you don't get to meet, your efforts show interest and initiative.

Whether you drop it off or mail it, always *include a cover letter.* (I'll talk about those in a minute.)

To Respond to Openings You Hear About Other Ways

Jobs get posted on company bulletin boards and job lines, or someone tells someone who tells you about an opening. Again, you can hand deliver your resume or mail it with a cover letter. If you heard about an opening through an electronic source, such as a website, follow the directions requested by the employer.

For example, in 1996 Advanced Micro Devices, Inc. was looking for a senior corporate counsel for their Austin, Texas, office. They gave three ways to submit your resume.

- You could use their Online Resume Form, which showed you how to format your resume for their scanning system.
- You could e-mail it.
- You could fax or mail it.

Most job openings I've seen give you these options. Even if you do e-mail or fax your resume, I'd also mail a copy that's printed on quality paper. (I go into more detail on electronic resumes in chapter seven.)

Recruiter Requests It

Mail it with a cover letter.

A Friend, Relative or Someone You Just Met Requests It

Thank them for their interest. Then ask, "What did you have in mind?"

If they say they want to pass it on to their son-in-law who owns a law firm in Chicago (where you want to move) and knows a lot of people, say: "That's terrific. If it's OK with you, I'd like to send it directly. Could you give me his name and address? It's my job search, and I wouldn't expect you to do my work for me. This way, I can also keep tabs on who has my resume, and I'll know whom I need to follow up with."

It's *possible* their son-in-law will read your resume and follow up. Chances are slim. Odds are greater it will get lost or he won't respond. Plus, unless he's looking for someone like you at the particular minute your resume arrives, what's he supposed to do with it?

I'm not a big fan of sending off resumes to people you don't know just because someone says it's a good idea. It's probably not such a good idea. It's more productive to get the son-in-law's name, write him a letter and see it he's willing to talk when you're in town. He could turn out to be a great source of information or even know companies that need your talents.

Bring your resume to the meeting. If you only talk on the phone, send him a copy after you hang up. *Remember, your goal is to get someone to take action with it.* If he knows you and likes you, he'll be more willing to do that.

Before or After an Informational Meeting

Again, an informational meeting is where you ask someone you know or you've been referred to to give you advice and information regarding your career. Depending on your situation, the purpose is to:

- Help you focus on an objective if you're not clear
- Get ideas on the types of positions you'd do well in
- Get ideas on the types of companies you could work for
- Be referred to other people who can also help you

If you talk to enough people, you may discover a position. People know information about their organizations and other people's companies and where openings are or will be coming up. So odds are pretty good that, eventually, someone will know someone who either has an opening or would see value in you and perhaps even create a position for you.

When you ask someone to take time to meet with you to get advice, you'll go in prepared to talk about yourself. Some people will want you to send a resume before the meeting.

If they don't request it beforehand, take it with you and leave it. It acts as your calling card in these situations.

This is another one of those times when people will say, "Give me a copy of your resume and I'll pass it around." Ask whom they were planning to give it to. Then explain, like you did to that well-meaning relative or friend, why it would be better if you could send it and follow up.

If There's No Known Opening

Like I said earlier, you can waste your time mailing off resumes to companies, hoping someone has an opening. It's like shooting an arrow into the sky with the message, "I'm available, do you have a job?" and hoping it will land in the hands of the right person. You've got better odds of winning the New York lottery. It would be smarter to aim your arrow to a known opening or change your message.

If you're interested in working for a particular industry or company, spend time holding informational meetings. Ask people you know what they know about the firm, what their needs are and where you might fit in. Ask if they know someone there you could talk to.

During Interviews and Phone Screenings

Your resume can give a prospective employer ideas about what to ask during the interview:

I see here you worked at the Loveland Plant for two years, then went to the Morris Foundation and came back to Loveland. What made you go back?

Or:

It says here you saved $150,000 by coming up with a new mailing system. How did you do that?

She may use it as a guide to walk through your various jobs or as a jumping off point: "Tell me more about the time you lived in Puerto Rico."

How it's used will depend on the interviewer.

The mere act of writing this type of marketing document will help *you* enormously in answering questions during the interview. That will get more clear in chapter two when I ask you for information about your life.

If you get a call from a company that wants to check you out on the phone before they schedule an interview, your resume can come in plenty handy. It will be full of little goodies about how well you performed in the past and describe your capabilities. And it should give a thorough overview of your experience and examples of how you applied your strengths.

So if the employer says, "Tell me about yourself," you've got everything you need right there in your hot little hands. Have it with you while you're on the phone. Use it as a guide. You should be thoroughly familiar with every word on it, but if it makes you feel more comfortable, use it. No one can see you.

To Fax or Not to Fax

When do you fax your resume? Only when someone says to. If she's not in a big hurry and the mail will do, mail it. It makes a better impression. Besides, fax paper gets all curled up, it's hard to read and the print eventually fades. Also, if you're sending your resume in confidence, you take the risk of others seeing it when you fax it.

SPEAKING OF COVER LETTERS

Please don't write letters that rehash your resume and go on for two and three pages.

Just grab my attention and get to the point of why you're interested in the position or want to talk to me. That should take a couple short paragraphs and *one* piece of paper.

Cover letters don't have to be stilted business babble. That goes for every word, from introduction to closing. Think about it like this: If you only had ten seconds, what would you say to the employer? Put *that* into words.

Avoid Ho-Hum Introductions

They go like this: "Please accept this letter as an application for the position you advertised in *The Miami Herald*. My resume is enclosed for your review."

Recent graduates have a tendency to start with, "I am a recent graduate of Northern Kentucky University where I majored in English." Sorry, but that will not make an employer jump out of her seat. You, especially, since you have little or no experience, must show—not tell—the employer your potential.

A young man who had just graduated and wanted a job as an advertising copywriter did that beautifully by handwriting a letter on a piece of cardboard.

(Granted, a more creative type can get away with this type of gimmick. At least this one did.) He also dribbled water on the ink to depict how teary-eyed he gets about his living situation. He wrote: "I'm currently living in a cardboard box. I spent all my savings on an envelope, postage and resume, so I decided to cut a window out of my wall." He said that although his living situation was tight, he had a portfolio and nice clothes and wanted to schedule an interview.

He not only got an interview at the advertising agency he sent this letter to, but the job as copywriter, too. The person who hired him told me, "We were looking for somebody who can come up with the big idea, the one that stands out from the crowd. He demonstrated that he knows what advertising is about: Get attention, get remembered and sell something."

Even if you're in the stuffiest of professions, you can learn from this example. Don't be afraid to be bold. Always be tasteful. But put yourself in the mind of the person you're writing to. Wake him up with an opening line that begs to be read. Keep him reading with the next sentence and the next one. Get him so curious about you, he'll have to meet you.

Avoid Saying Nothing

The meat of many cover letters goes on to say: "I am very excited about the opportunity your company is offering. I am people oriented, have experience with computers and am looking to build on my experience. I believe I have the skills to excel at this job."

Employers don't hire to give you an opportunity or build on your experience. Second, they don't care what you believe. They want to know what you can do for them.

Avoid Ending on a Predictable Note

Most letters end with, "I would appreciate the chance to discuss the position, as it sounds like a great opportunity. I look forward to hearing from you." This is not only blasé, monotonous and dull, but sends two wrong messages. One, you want the company to give you a great opportunity. This, as you know, is not what they're in business for. Two, you're not interested enough to follow up.

When I interviewed management expert and author Tom Peters for my radio program, he told me how he had just hired someone in a manager's position for a small start-up company he's involved in.

I got 200 resumes, but she made the short list immediately because she had a good-looking letterhead with a terrific logo, and the letter began, 'You don't need to look any further to fill this job at your company.' I liked that audacity. Obviously, if she'd had a rotten resume, that audacity wouldn't have gotten her anywhere. I was amazed that of the 200 applications I got, excuse the blunt language, but 175 of them were crap in terms of personal presentation. Almost all of them had good backgrounds, but they didn't present themselves well in that written document, which is obviously the first thing I'm going to see.

And do go to the trouble of finding out the names of the people you're writing to and their genders if they have names like Chris, Kim or Terry, which could be male or female.

You'll not only stand out from the crowd who tends to write salutations such as "Dear Gentleman," "Dear Sir" or "To Whom It May Concern," but you show initiative and don't risk insulting anyone.

"When I get letters addressed to 'Mr.' Ravenna, they go straight in the trash," *Ms.* Ravenna, who does the hiring in her department, told me. Another person, who works for Edward Howard & Company, a public relations firm in Akron, Ohio, told me she gets letters addressed to Mr. Edward and Mr. Howard and Mr. Edward Howard. Mr. Edward never existed, and Mr. Edward Howard died years ago.

A friend of mine ran an ad in the newspaper for a position at his company and got seventy-eight responses. The salutations included Dear Sir/Madam, To Whom It May Concern, Dear Personnel, Attention Human Resources, Dear Recruitment Manager, To Whom, To Whom This May Concern, Gentlemen, Dear Employer and, my favorite, Hi! Not one person bothered to get a name.

Of course, if the ad is blind, that is, there is no company name, you're stuck with a more generic salutation. Following are a few sample cover letters that do the job just fine.

EIGHT THINGS PEOPLE WASTE TIME WORRYING ABOUT

There's only one thing you need to think about when you sit down to write your resume. And it's none of these.

1. Who Might Read Your Resume and What They'll Think

You can't possibly know everyone who will read it. And you certainly can't predict how they will all react. Everyone will be different.

Someone told me a story of how, after just completing his resume, he held an informational meeting with an attorney. "The attorney began picking my resume apart. 'You can't *contribute* a background,' she told me. 'And this word here is redundant. And I think this looks too busy here. You should change this. . . .' "

Someone may have legitimate feedback. Although in this case, and most other times, I find people just like to voice their opinions.

If you feel good about your resume, thank the person for her input and trust your instincts. And don't ask everyone else what they think.

Concentrate on the four things most people expect. Don't waste time trying to please everyone and wondering what they'll think. You'll never know. Concentrate on what *you* want them to know.

2. Whether You Should Write a Resume for Each Job You Apply For

Only do this if you have nothing better to do with your time. If your resume is done right, it will reflect who you are and the kind of work you do. So you don't need to write a resume for each job you apply for. Your cover letter can address the specifics of the job.

If you're only applying for one position at one company and nowhere else, you can certainly tailor it to what you know about the position or the industry. This would also make sense for those times you're not really looking for a position and don't have an updated version but hear about something that you'd like to apply for.

Some people still like to tweak a thing or two to customize theirs for a particular job. Others are pursuing a couple different directions. In those cases, you will probably have different resumes. But

Sample cover letter

JULIE GENERIC

111 St. Paul Street
Atlanta, Georgia 30344
(770) 421-4986

September 9, 1997

Ms. Joy Ephart
The Loganizer Accounting & Consulting Firm
50 S. Wedge Avenue
Minneapolis, Minnesota 55422

Dear Ms. Ephart:

If you're looking for a dynamic and energetic leader to help you meet your increasing demand for consulting services, you won't find anyone more qualified than I am.

I have a twelve-year proven track record in financial operations and management as a consultant in a Big Eight accounting firm in the areas of controlling, financial planning and analysis and financial systems and operations.

My expertise includes business restructuring, operations improvements, market analysis, process reengineering and accounting systems.

My communications skills are finely tuned, and I have developed a reputation for building trusting relationships.

If you would like to know more about how my leadership skills and in-depth knowledge of financial planning and analysis can be an asset to The Loganizer Accounting & Consulting Firm, let's talk.

I will be in Minneapolis October 15-20. I will call you next week.

Sincerely,

Julie Generic

Sample cover letter

JOAN FONTANA

1100 Liquid Circle
Seattle, Washington 98104

December 5, 1997

Mr. Lama Lorenzo
Director
Michigan Library Foundation
5555 Libra Way
Troy, Michigan 48084

Dear Mr. Lorenzo:

The challenges the Michigan Library Foundation face are exactly the kind of problems an experienced marketer like me has a proven record in solving.

As the marketing director of three other nonprofit agencies, I have turned around these struggling organizations into thriving foundations.

You can see by reading my resume how closely I've worked with the media to make a dramatic difference that led to strong member support. My skills and knowledge in stakeholder communications has also been a key to my success. Other strengths include my ability to:

- Create long-range marketing plans
- Develop sound public relations programs
- Formulate effective communications to motivate targeted audiences
- Lead diverse team members to consensus
- Conduct extensive market research

If you would like to see the Michigan Library Foundation develop into a self-supporting organization with a strong member base, I can help you reach that goal. I will call you next week to arrange an interview.

Thank you.

Sincerely,

Joan Fontana

in general, if you're focusing on one area, you don't need to write a resume for every job.

3. Whether It Should Be One, Two or Three Pages

If you've got two pages of fantastic information that tell about your fifteen years of record accomplishments, are you going to *not* include half this fascinating information because you heard somewhere, "Resumes are supposed to be one page"?

This "resumes-should-be-one-page" rule got started because people read or heard somewhere that employers only spend about twenty seconds looking at a resume. Therefore, they concluded that all resumes should be one page. Think about how ridiculous this logic is.

Assuming people do spend only about twenty seconds on a resume, if yours is one page, does that mean it will get more than twenty seconds of attention? Or because yours is one page, will it get read in twenty seconds? In other words, do one-page resumes help people speed-read? Or because it looks short, will it get read from top to bottom? Of course not, to all three scenarios.

People are skimmers. Especially if someone received your resume along with ninety others in the mail, yours and everyone else's might get a once-over whether it's one, two or three pages. The reader is looking for key pieces of information that grab attention and influence her to put you in the keeper or trash pile.

Now some people have an aversion to resumes that are more than one page. They may refuse to read anything but a one-pager. That's their problem. They could be missing out on the next Albert Einstein because of this arbitrary rule.

People in the music industry will tell you that for a song to get air play on the radio, it should be three minutes long. Remember "Hey Jude" by the Beatles? It ran seven minutes and fifteen seconds. It was the number one song in the U.S., Britain and ten other countries. It was recorded by hundreds of other artists including Chet Atkins, Count Basie, Petula Clark, Bing Crosby, Elvis and, of course, Muzak.

The typical symphony always had four movements, averaged twenty-five to thirty minutes in length and only used orchestral music. That is until 1824 when Ludwig van Beethoven premiered his ninth symphony. It had four movements, but they were more complex than those in the conventional symphony. It used choral and vocal soloists and was seventy minutes long. This had *never* been done before. Why the drastic deviation from the norm? Beethoven had something more to convey, and just using the orchestra wasn't going to cut it. He needed text and human voices. He followed the symphonic form but had to go beyond it.

Movies are "supposed to be" no more than two hours. *Schindler's List* was over three hours and received eight Oscars out of twelve nominations.

When great movies, music or whatever are being conceived, their creators don't start out with a list of "should bes." They start with *visions of what they want the works to be*. What they want them to communicate. What they want the viewer, listener or reader to feel or understand. Yes, the end result will fit into a format of some kind. But the format is a guide, not a dictator.

I'm not suggesting you write a resume that will make it into *The Guinness Book of Records* for the world's longest resume. Yes, you'll be writing a resume that fits a general format or combination of formats. Yes, you want to keep it brief and succinct. (We'll talk about that in chapter five.) But your goal is not to create a one-page resume. It's to create a dynamic marketing tool. So bust out of your limited thinking.

4. How You're Going to Deal With That Gap in Your Job History

No one has a perfect career. This is one of those facts of life that you'll either figure out a way to downplay or not worry about. It's not going to make or break your success. And if someone shuns you because of a gap in your work history, then they've got their priorities wrong.

I know people who took time off from their "traditional" career path to hitchhike across the U.S., write poetry, be a bricklayer in Dallas or a nanny to a family in Paris, France. They came back richer in real-world experiences, more emotionally mature, more well rounded and filled with a wealth of experience they couldn't have gotten sitting in some office. Many people will appreciate that.

On the other hand, if you have been out of the

workforce for a while, for example, raising a family, looking for a new job for over a year, or working in an unrelated field, you may have to help overcome an employer's concern that your knowledge is outdated, you don't know the technology or you aren't familiar with how things run in the business world. (We'll discuss this in chapter six.) But you don't need to lose sleep over it.

5. How to Deal With the Fact That You Have No Experience

Paid experience isn't everything. Besides, employers don't expect you to have it if you're just out of school. If you're switching careers, you do have experience; it's just in a different area. So you have to concentrate on your skills and how they transfer and demonstrate your potential. (Chapter six talks about this.)

6. How to Deal With the Fact That You're Over Fifty

What does that have to do with anything? In chapter six we'll discuss how to downplay this if you're concerned. But don't let it be an obstacle in developing your resume. It may just be something you consider when deciding what experience or dates to include or leave out.

7. How to Handle the Fact That You Were Fired or Quit Your Last Job

How would that come up in your resume anyway?

8. How to Handle the Fact That All Your Experience Was in Nonprofit Organizations or Education or With One Company

So what? Quit worrying about things you have no control over. Quit thinking you need to write your resume from a defensive position. When you do, writing a resume is a dim and depressing chore. And that kind of resume is definitely not going to do its job. If you're really concerned about this, I do give ideas on how to deal with it in chapter six.

GET ONE AND ONE THING ONLY ON YOUR MIND

That one thing is, *What do you want your resume to do for you?*

That's simple, you say. To get me a job.

Run that by me again. Did you say you want your resume to get you a job? If that's your answer, you have a problem. A big one. No one *gives you a job*.

Now if you're sitting there saying, "I know that, that's not what I meant," hold on a second.

If you think your resume will answer all your prayers, you really don't understand what this whole resume business is about. And if you're serious about getting the job you want, understanding this point is crucial. So let's make this perfectly clear.

To get the job you want, *you must prove to employers that you have the skills, knowledge and background to solve their problems and to improve their lives.*

That's *all* an employer cares about when she's hiring. She doesn't care that you want a job, need a job, would love a job with her company, will sweep floors to get a job.

Look, she doesn't even know you exist. Then one day, there's your resume on her desk. It must now jump up and shout, "Check me out. I'm the one who can do what you need, who can solve your problems!"

So, back to my point about the only thing you need to think about when you sit down to write your resume. That one thing is, What do you want your resume to do for you? Stumped? Let me give you some ideas.

Is it to present yourself as a take-charge leader who turns unprofitable business operations into highly efficient and productive organizations? Then *that's* what should be uppermost in your mind when you write your resume.

Is it to show someone that you can be the most talented performer their musical group has ever known and can entertain and charm the pants off an audience? Then, start there.

Is it to show a radio program director you have the talent and skill to be the next Rush Limbaugh or Howard Stern?

Four months before the 1996 presidential election, there was an article on the front page of *The Cincinnati Enquirer* about Ohio's governor, George Voinovich. The headline read, "Governor Voinovich Polishes Image as OHIO'S MR. FIX-IT."

At that time, he was being considered as a running mate of presidential hopeful Bob Dole and pos-

Resume Collectors			
	WHY THEY WANT IT	**WHAT THEY LOOK FOR**	**WHAT THEY DO WITH YOUR RESUME**
RECRUITERS	Have position to fill; want to screen you	• Job stability • Career continuity • Professionalism: grammar, typos, neatness • Competency in key areas	• File it • Put it in database • Throw it away • Call you
HUMAN RESOURCE PROFESSIONALS	Have position to fill; want to screen you	• Job stability • Career continuity • Professionalism: grammar, typos, neatness • Competency in key areas	• File it • Throw it away • Refer to someone • Follow up
OTHER PEOPLE IN COMPANIES	Know of definite or future opening	• Job stability • Career continuity • Professionalism: grammar, typos, neatness • Competency in key areas	• File it • Throw it away • Refer to someone • Follow up
FRIENDS, FAMILY AND OTHER WELL-MEANING FOLKS	Think they can refer you to someone	• Job stability • Career continuity • Professionalism: grammar, typos, neatness • Competency in key areas • If you've had decent jobs	• File it • Throw it away • Refer to someone • Follow up • Stick it in a drawer at home

sibly as a candidate for the U.S. Senate. The article cited several examples of how he has created this "Mr. Fix-it" image, like the time he got top executives to be a part of a task force to scrutinize government operations, resulting in the elimination of unnecessary boards and commissions, paring the number of civil servants and privatizing parts of city and state government.

This is what's called "positioning." *Positioning* is a term coined by communications consultant Jack Trout in 1969 to describe, as he says, not what you do to the product, but what you do to the *mind*.

People's minds are limited, says Trout in his book *The New Positioning*. They can't cope with the mountains of information. Plus, minds hate confusion. So you need to oversimplify your message. Governor Voinovich simplified his message and positioned himself as "Mr. Fix-it."

So how do you want your resume to position you? What's the one, simple message you want employers to get about you? What idea do you want to get across? That's what I mean when I say, "What do you want your resume to do for you?" Are you with me?

Fill in the blank below. Then, when you're ready to write your resume, go back to this statement and use it as a guide. When you finish your resume, check to see if you've communicated that message.

When an employer reads my resume, he or she will see me as _____

_____

_____

_____

Your resume is a vehicle for delivering that message.

All this other malarkey about age, gaps in work history, whether it should be one or two pages will take you off track from your objective, which is: To hook and hold the attention of employers and show them you have the potential to improve their lives.

You will get your next job. Your resume is a tool to get you there. A tool that the world requires. A tool that you have complete freedom to create (staying within the bounds of truth, of course).

Just focus on what you want that busy businessperson to know about you and what you can do for her.

SUMMARY

- You need a resume to introduce yourself to a big world full of incredibly busy people.
- A resume that will get employers excited about meeting you must show them you have the potential to improve their lives.
- Everyone expects you to have a resume.
- Even though most everyone will ask for yours, don't necessarily give it to them.
- You can't write a resume that will satisfy everyone; you can only create a resume that satisfies you and deals with the four basic things people look for: What can you do? Have you done it and stuck with it? What do you know? What kind of person are you?
- There are no absolute rules for writing a resume except to be strategic: Pick and choose information that supports your career objective. Think through the best place to put that information. Be selective with the words you choose.
- The only thing to think about when you sit down to write your resume is, What do I want this resume to do? Concentrate on the one, simple message you want people to know about you. Focus on how you can improve their lives.

chapter two

First Things First: The Facts, Just the Facts

You're not writing anything yet. You and I are going to think out loud for awhile and jot down some notes—about your life, what you've been doing for the last umpteen years, what kind of stuff you know about, how knowledgeable you are and what makes you so special. Well, you are, you know. No one else has your perspective, experiences and personality.

And that's what this chapter is going to wangle out of you. It's the kind of data that will eventually go on your resume. Information that shows those four things most everyone wants to know:

- What can you do?
- Have you done it and stuck with it?
- What do you know?
- What kind of person are you?

For now, we're not worrying about how it's written, what order things happened in, whether a job or project was the coolest thing you ever did, whether or not your boss liked it or if you left a particular job for a better offer or were given the boot unfairly. We're just getting the facts.

This is like creating your favorite dish. Take for instance, chicken curry (which is one of mine). If you were going to make it for dinner, you'd need chicken, of course. Then you'd go to your cup-

boards and pull out flour, thyme, curry powder, green peppers, onion and stewed tomatoes and set them all on the counter. These are your ingredients. Later you'll mix them all together in a particular order. Depending on how spicy you like your chicken curry, you might add a larger quantity of a certain spice or even improvise.

We're going to do the same thing with the ingredients for your resume. We'll lay out a lot of pertinent information on paper and see what we have to work with. We may not use it all. We may even spice up some information. Basically, we're going to brain dump. So get out more paper to write on or use the worksheets provided here.

WHAT WE'RE DIGGING FOR
Your strengths

Hold it right here, and make sure you know what those are. Most people don't. They think they do, but when I ask them to tell me the six to eight skills they enjoy using most and are most effective in applying, they say something like this:

Well, I'm a people person. Hmmm . . . I'm good at analyzing. Let's see . . . I'm uhh, dependable. Ummm, I like to help people. Is that six?

Not exactly what I had in mind. Strengths are those skills that tell precisely what you *do* well. They are the things you love to do and that come to you naturally. They're words like *write, organize, plan, present, monitor, follow through, analyze, lead, problem solve, coordinate, research, train.*

You get the idea. They're not just any old skills you might have, mind you. They're the ones you are most motivated to do and enjoy using. They're one of the major reasons someone wants to hire you.

If you're not sure what your strengths are, you absolutely, positively, without hesitation must figure them out. They're ultra, ultra important. They are the foundation for the rest of the resume. They're like the chicken in my chicken curry recipe (or tofu if you're a vegetarian).

Here's an exercise to help you identify your strengths. I'll walk you through it here, and then you can fill out the worksheet on page 21.

1. Write down events, projects or situations that you've been involved in and are proud of, enjoyed doing and that have some type of result. These would be accomplishments. Things you feel good about. Forget about whether someone else thinks they were great events.

Just write a few sentences. Here are examples:

- I created an advertising campaign for an industrial client that generated such enormous numbers of leads that the company met its annual sales goals in three months.
- I developed a training program for 300 managers and staff members of a diverse workforce on multicultural issues. The program became the benchmark for diversity training in major companies across the country.
- I oversaw a lease financing deal between several large equipment manufacturers and resellers that opens up a new realm of customers and significantly increases our customer base.
- I developed spreadsheets that clearly illustrated annual spending trends and cost allocations.
- I coordinated a grassroots campaign and developed a political strategy that resulted in the highest percentage of votes ever recorded in

the city's history to defeat an earnings tax; it saved taxpayers $12 million.
- I evaluated a 42-year-old male who was overweight and depressed. I created a program that included regimented exercise, new diet and counseling that led to considerable weight loss and happier personal relationships.
- I initiated an adult study group that researches and discusses ecological concerns; the group has raised $5,000 to develop a bird sanctuary.
- I raised money to start a volunteer clinic to serve a neighborhood of 10,000 citizens who had no health care. Today the clinic has 60 paid staff members and serves 15,000 people.
- I was one of 25 students who won an award in a nationwide science and technology competition for a robot I designed.

(By the way, the last five accomplishments were done in a volunteer capacity.)

You don't have to say a lot. Like the examples I just listed, describe the situation, what you did and the result of your efforts.

2. Next, figure out what skills it took to accomplish each example you list. Let's look at the first example, the advertising campaign, that my client created. Here's some of what he had to do:

conceptualize
research
organize
plan
write
present
persuade
envision
motivate
create
communicate
negotiate
coordinate

Of course there's more. But you get my drift.

3. Do this for as many accomplishments as you can think of—the more the better. Break each one down by the skills it took to accomplish it.

4. Make a master list of all these words.

5. Now prioritize this list of words according to

Exercise to Determine Your Strengths

1. Write down events, projects or situations you enjoyed doing and are proud of that had some type of result. These are accomplishments. For examples see page 20.

_____
_____
_____
_____
_____
_____
_____
_____
_____
_____
_____
_____
_____

2. Write down the skills it took to accomplish each of the above examples.

_____
_____
_____
_____
_____
_____
_____

3. Make a master list of all the above words then decide what you enjoy doing the most by prioritizing the words according to enjoyment.

_____
_____
_____
_____
_____
_____

4. Define the top six to eight words further to determine what each really means to you. These phrases describe your strengths.

_____
_____
_____
_____
_____
_____

what you enjoy most. Look at the list and say, "If I had to choose the *one* thing I enjoy doing most out of all of these, what would it be? What do I like doing second best? Third best?"

6. Look at the six to eight words that you enjoy most. Most likely, these will be your strengths.

7. There's one more thing you need to do. Let's say some of your strengths are write, analyze and research. That could mean anything. But what does it mean to *you*? Do you like to write news articles? Or do you like to write proposals? Or advertising copy? Do you like to analyze financial data or people's behavior? They're very different. Do you like to research medical facts, historical information or what? So now you need to define those words further.

You'll end up with six to eight phrases that describe your strongest skills—your strengths.

For example, after this client went through the exercise, here are the phrases that describe his stongest skills:

- Conceive and implement persuasive political and marketing strategies
- Promote products, policies and services
- Write and communicate concepts, proposals and plans
- Create marketing and communications programs
- Research and analyze marketing data

Proof

If you thought you could skip that last exercise, here's why you can't. You have to know what your strengths are if you're going to show proof. Why are examples so important? Let's say I've got a job to fill. So I want someone with particular skills. Just because you tell me you have these skills isn't going to cut it. I want proof. So you need to give me examples. You'll list your best examples (or ones that support your career objective) as accomplishments or achievements on your resume. This will be one of the most important ingredients of your resume. Use the chart on page 24 to list your examples now.

It's information that answers the employers' questions: How will you improve my life? How will you make my business better? How will you improve productivity or cut costs? How will you help

STRENGTH	PROOF
Develop procedures	I initiated a procedure to reduce production costs for our company. It ended up saving us $12,000 annually.
Analyze communication needs	I spearheaded a corporate communication program that increased our company revenues despite a market downturn.
Create promotional campaigns	I created a telemarketing and promotional campaign that increased group membership in our organization by 50% and revenues by 30% in a highly competitive market.
Liaison between government and community	I oversaw a lobbying campaign that was directed to legislators. It resulted in the state's commitment to build a $100 million highway.
Conceive innovative programs	I created the "online card" program, a value-added service that gives consumers rebates on goods and services at participating merchants, including grocery stores, restaurants and car dealers.

us stay competitive? How will you make us the leader in our industry? Yes, these are the reasons they hire you in the first place.

See above and next page for examples of how others proved their ability to keep their organizations competitive or make something better.

I know the examples in this chart seem bare bones. That's because they are. They started out as wordy, detailed descriptions my clients wrote when I told them to come up with examples of how they've used the particular skills. We diluted them down to

STRENGTH	PROOF
Manage daily operations	I maintained a smooth flow of operations during a remodeling project of a 200,000-square-foot facility over a three-month period.
Negotiate contracts	I negotiated a contract with an external laboratory for the best price for our three participating hospitals.
Analyze business operations	After analyzing a wholesale business, I chose and implemented an integrated management and accounting system that resulted in $10 million in revenues over four years.
Motivate others to reach goals and objectives	I motivated my fellow students to volunteer for a fund-raising event that generated $3,000 for the Heart Association.
Train adults	I designed and presented training for new African-American employees that facilitated their understanding of the corporate culture and significantly hastened their acclimation time.
Leadership	I founded a legal advocacy resource group in which attorneys act on behalf of thousands of children involved in abuse and neglect cases.

Where You Worked and When

Write the *complete* name of the company and city and state you worked in. You don't need to give the street address or your supervisor's name. List the division you worked in, if applicable.

If you worked in several positions, write the years you were in each job. No, you don't need months you worked there.

If you worked at the same company most or all of your career, write down the years you worked there, then break down the years at the various positions (see last example below).

Examples:

- Menashe's Eatery, Brooklyn, New York 1984-1996
- Evi & Al's Dental Lab, Inc., Cleveland, Ohio 1976-1990
- Florence International Corporation, San Francisco, California 1990-Present
- Shana Middle School, Paris Public School System, Paris, Kentucky 1970-1990
- The Ohio State University, College of Dentistry, Columbus, Ohio 1988
- The Procter and Gamble Company, Cincinnati, Ohio 1976-1996
    - Chemist   1986-1996
    - Lab Manager   1981-1985
    - Lab Technician   1976-1980

Company name	City	State	Years
_____	_____	_____	_____
_____	_____	_____	_____
_____	_____	_____	_____
_____	_____	_____	_____
_____	_____	_____	_____
_____	_____	_____	_____

What in the World Do They Do?

The E.G. Wilson Company doesn't mean hooey to most people. So a brief description of what the company makes, sells or does tells somebody whether you worked for a steel company or a counseling service and sometimes even the scope or size of the organization.

the important information: what they did and what the end results for the companies or organizations were—in other words, how these actions made something better. You can always give more detail in the interview. But your resume is the place for brevity and hard-hitting facts.

Examples of how I've used my strengths effectively (proof):

1. _____
   _____
   _____
   _____

2. _____
   _____
   _____
   _____

3. _____
   _____
   _____
   _____

4. _____
   _____
   _____
   _____

5. _____
   _____
   _____
   _____

6. _____
   _____
   _____

You may need to define the particular division you worked for. Companies in foreign lands have names that won't be easily recognizable. Some company names can be deceiving. For instance, what would you think Cincinnati Restoration, Inc. does? Remodeling? They are a mental health agency that works with severely mentally handicapped adults. (By the way, they have since changed their name.)

Even if you're a dentist—something that everyone knows about—you can write a description that tells what type of practice you work in. (See second example.)

Examples of company descriptions:

- E.G. Wilson Company, manufacturer and distributor of lubricants, industrial metalworking and fuels.
- Dr. Morris Armstrong, dental family practice that treats up to 2,000 patients and includes cosmetic and implant dentistry.
- *The Cincinnati Enquirer*, major metropolitan daily newspaper with circulation of 550,000.
- WYUB, one of the top public radio stations in U.S. with annual budget of over $1.5 million.
- The Procter and Gamble Company, global Fortune 500 consumer products manufacturer.
- Sam & Edith Steel Company, a major steel producer with sales in excess of $1.3 billion.
- Vera's Gallery, a gallery and gift shop specializing in handcrafted goods.
- Reed Services, a nonprofit agency that provides food and clothing for the needy.
- Rinky Dink Management, a property management firm operating six apartment complexes in the Louisville area.

Company & description	Product it makes/service it offers	Sales volume/ budget
_____	_____	_____
_____	_____	_____
_____	_____	_____
_____	_____	_____

What Do They Call You, and What Do You Do All Day?

List the title you had at the company. If it's one of those titles that would be gibberish to someone outside the company, like Auditor One, Level 2 or B.O.F. Caster, write an alternative title that's more generic. Now don't come unglued about altering this.

Remember, you're trying to create a marketing document that conveys meaning to the reader. It's not doing that if someone looks at your title and wonders, "What in the world is a Gribbendobber?"

Don't misrepresent yourself either. If you were a supervisor in customer service, don't say you were a manager. Or if you were a manager, don't put director. If you worked in a specific division, write that down.

Examples:

- Directory of Quality
- Administrative Assistant, Office of the President
- Assistant Superintendent
- Nurse Technician, Emergency Services
- Computer Support Specialist
- Manager, Management Systems

You also need to describe what you do or what kinds of gizmos and gadgets you work with. If you're not sure how to describe your job, pull out your job description or check the *Dictionary of Occupational Titles*, a very thick 1,915-page reference book published by the Department of Labor. It will give you language for most all types of jobs. Check the library.

Don't use passive language, such as "Responsible for operations." Sit down and really examine the activities you're involved in every day. Use active words such as *lead, write, oversee, manage, present, handle, create, interpret, analyze.* (More on this in chapter five.)

EXAMPLES OF HOW PEOPLE DESCRIBE THEIR JOBS:

Lead development of quality systems and productivity improvement in operations and product development.

Oversee operations for 250-student elementary school with 40 teachers and 20 support staff members.

Created and implemented information system strategies.

Handled daily operations including bookkeeping, inventory and record keeping.

Oversee interactive, multimedia and website development for marketing programs.

Plan, coordinate and design World Wide Web sites.

Developed operating procedures. Organized and coordinated merchandising and display windows.

Developed internal procedures to keep databases up-to-date and accurate; proofread text.

Interpreted regulatory and hazard requirements of certifying boards. Developed standard operating procedures and maintained revisions and updates. Performed internal and external quality system audits.

Oversaw sales in three-state area.

Managed flow of daily inventory, revenue and accounting system. Planned and organized office moves.

Design research studies for 25 national clients in packaged goods, financial services, health care and telecommunications industries.

Manage computing and network infrastructure and application support.

Conduct diversity training.

Handle up to $3 million in sales.

Oversee $400,000 operations budget.

EXAMPLES OF YOUR EXPERTISE IN A NUTSHELL:

Manufacturing and hands-on experience in new product development, information systems and quality

Twenty years in the operation and maintenance of water treatment equipment

Hands-on and educational experience in health services administration in U.S. and Europe

Five years' study and practical hands-on experience in financial sales and service

Over ten years in business-to-business, industrial and consumer promotion and politics

Five years' experience in direct sales and product promotion

Fifteen years in marketing research and management

Eight years in operations and retail management

Twelve years in legal research and case preparation

Sixteen years' experience in mechanical patent practice

Twenty years in financial management and operations management

Strategic planning development, acquisitions and divestitures

Semiconductor engineering and manufacturing

Electrical engineering and technical field services

Cost estimating and scheduling of construction projects

Six years in sales administration and customer service in the insurance industry

Bookkeeping and data entry

Broadcasting, including radio, television and cable, announcing, recording and editing, programming, sales and audio/video production

Financial analysis and strategic planning and management

Also, when you can, give the scope of your responsibilities. For example, if you're a secretary, you can include the number of executives you worked for; an executive can give the budgets she handled; a salesperson, the size of his sales territory or number of clients he served.

Your title	What you do or did
_____	_____
_____	_____
_____	_____
_____	_____
_____	_____

Your Expertise in a Nutshell

This is a phrase or two that captures the breadth of your experience. Think about it like this: If you had to explain what you've been doing for the last umpteen years in a single sentence, how would you describe it?

Even if you're a recent graduate, you can come up with this. More colleges today require internships and cooperative experience. Use these. (See the third and fourth examples.)

If you have experience in several areas, combine them in a statement or two.

Summary of your experience

_____

_____

_____

_____

Whaddaya Know?

People always look at me strangely when I tell them to write down everything they know about. "Whaddaya mean, write down everything I know about?" they say. I mean just that. But since this is a book on resumes, keep your list focused on everything you know about related to your career, education, experience and special interests. (If this was a book on career change, I would not limit it.)

This is knowledge you've developed from your experience and training, subjects you're familiar with but are not necessarily an expert on, plus information you *are* an expert on. Depending on your field and how long you've been working, this can be a lengthy list.

EXAMPLES OF WHAT OTHER PEOPLE KNOW ABOUT:

Finance, forecasting and development of statistical reports

Intellectual property transactions, litigation management, acquisitions and joint ventures

Demographics related to trends, population, employment, gender, race and age distribution

Financial impact of racism and diversity

Census analysis and research

Management and human resources, including hiring, retention, performance appraisals, mentoring

Curriculum development and training

Thorough understanding of tele-communications and information superhighway

Petro chemical products, including lubricants, oils, fats and fuels

Raw materials and blending processes

Chemical reactivities and flammabilities

EPA, OSHA and NAFTA regulations

Quality systems, including customer surveys, control charts, statistical process control, auditing

ISO9001 quality system standard

Hazardous material reporting systems

New business ventures

Imports and exports

Personnel management, affirmative action, unions, compensation

All facets of manufacturing operations

Patient care, medications, monitoring IVs, bedside patient care, including ADLs, treatments and care planning

EXAMPLES OF WHAT OTHER PEOPLE KNOW ABOUT:

Budgets, project coordination, training, management

Word processing, Lotus 1-2-3, spreadsheets

Vendor relations, publishing production process, scheduling, pricing, order fulfillment

Regulatory affairs, unions, forecasting

Biofeedback, massage therapy and shiatsu massage, meditation, yoga, tai chi and aikido

Aerobics, weight training, body building, weight loss, injury prevention

Nutrition, including vitamins, vegetarianism, macrobiotics

Trade shows, special events, speech writing, editing, proposal development, script writing, direct mail, media relations, advertising, fund-raising, grant writing

Environment and conservation

Payroll, taxes, business valuation, auditing and internal control procedures

Inventory control, supervision

Women's issues, working task forces, volunteer recruitment, workshop development and presentation

French and Spanish languages and cultures

Issues related to people with mental and physical disabilities

Everything you know about

_____
_____
_____
_____
_____
_____
_____
_____
_____
_____

Are You Educated?

Write down degrees, where you studied, continuing education classes and dates. If you've had dozens of continuing education classes through your company and there are too many to list or titles won't mean anything to someone else, write general categories, such as management, communication, quality and diversity. Ask your human resource department for a list of courses you've taken over the years. In the future, keep track of this information in a file at home.

Even if you didn't complete your degree, write down the courses or general areas of study and where and when you were a student. List internships and cooperative education work experiences.

Examples of education:

- CPA Certificate 1979
- Master of Business Administration, Xavier University 1982
- Master of Public Administration 1990
- B.A. Journalism, Minor in Women's Studies, Kent State University 1988
- General business courses toward attainment of Associates in Business Administration, Lane Community College 1968
- Certified Financial Planner Designation; Licenses include: Series 63, 65
- Continuing education includes Total Quality Management and Interaction Management
- Graduate studies in Psychology, University of Wisconsin 1980-1982
- Tai Chi training
- Certified Apartment Maintenance Technician

Your education

_____
_____
_____
_____

Do You Belong to Professional Groups?

Write out memberships, affiliations and offices you held with professional and trade organizations you belong to.

Examples of memberships:

- American College of Healthcare Executives
- Alabama Society of Radiologic Technologists

- Women in Communications
- American Institute of Certified Public Accountants
- American Society of Journalists and Authors
- Public Relations Society of America
- Sales and Marketing Executives
    President and past Director of Membership
- Public Relations Student Society of America
- Student Association of Manufacturing Engineers

Your memberships, affiliations and offices you held

_____
_____
_____
_____
_____
_____
_____

Are You a Joiner?

Include organizations you belong to and socially redeeming endeavors you participate in, offices you've held or still hold that are not necessarily related to your profession.

Examples of organizations:

- Phi Beta Kappa
- National Honor Society
- Volunteer for Oktoberfest
- Chairperson, United Way Campaign
- Chair of Communications Committee, March of Dimes
- Blue Chip Campaign for City Downtown Development
- Big Brothers/Big Sisters
- Junior Achievement
- Spalding College Alumni Club
- Track team

Your activities

_____
_____
_____
_____
_____

Oscars and Other Recognition

List awards and other recognition you've received with, possibly, a brief explanation of why it's significant.

Examples of recognition:

- 1995 Who's Who of American Business Leaders
- 1994 YWCA Career Woman of Achievement
- 1996 Addy Award for Best Newspaper Ad Category/Copywriting and Art Direction
- Junior Achievement Advisor of Year
- 1997 Woman of the Year

Recognition you've received

_____
_____
_____
_____

Habla Español?

Do you speak other languages besides English? Simply list your expertise:

Speak fluent Chinese and English

Languages you speak

_____
_____
_____

How the World Sees You

Employers want to know what you can do, but also what kind of person you are. Today, companies emphasize customer service, flexibility, team orientation and ability to solve problems. So you'll see more employers examining the way you think, grow, communicate and approach your work.

You can give them a sense of these things by describing your personality, how you handle situations, what you're known for and what kind of reputation you've developed.

Write down words and phrases that describe this. If you're stuck, ask others how they'd describe you. Look back at your achievements you analyzed, and think of words that describe how you did those things.

EXAMPLES OF HOW OTHERS DESCRIBE YOU:

Known as an astute troubleshooter with the ability to analyze and design efficient internal systems

Known for ability to instill "can-do" attitude in others

Persuasive leader who can achieve bottom-line results

Ability to garner support from others

Take-charge leader

Skilled liaison

Perceptive and good listener

Committed, conscientious, goal oriented

Diplomatic, efficient minded

Resourceful in handling emergencies and deadlines

Highly creative, self-motivated and empathetic

How others describe you

_____
_____
_____
_____
_____
_____

GETTING PERSONAL

You'll notice I didn't have you list personal information like whether you're married, how many kids you have or what church or synagogue you belong to. This information has nothing to do with whether you're qualified for a job. So I wouldn't put it on a resume.

What about hobbies? Well, do any of them make you a more desirable worker? Someone usually brings to my attention that if you put down "Golf" as one of your activities, for example, it might spark an interest by the person looking at your resume. Then they go on to tell me how that very listing of "Golf" turned into a friendly conversation once they were in the interview.

Well, I suppose that can happen. But it's quite a reach to conclude that just because you play golf or rugby someone will be interested in you as an employee. Sure it might generate conversation or establish commonality between you and an interviewer. On the other hand, the person looking at the resumes might also care less about golf, rugby or that you're on a bowling league.

I'd stay away from listing political or religious affiliations or reference to your race. That is, unless it will be beneficial in some way.

There's a fine line here. The fact that you ran in the Chicago Marathon for three years might be evidence of commitment, determination and self-discipline—qualities that are important to doing a job. Use your judgment.

My general rule is to ask yourself, Does this information have anything to do with my ability to do the job or show my potential? If not, leave it off.

When you're writing your resume, you may decide that some of the information you did list in this chapter also has nothing to do with whether you're qualified for a job, or is just something you'd rather not share. However, the categories I've listed here have the potential to be applicable. Your marital status, religious affiliation and number of children are just plain irrelevant.

LAST WORDS

Alrighty. Now you should have all of the potential ingredients of your resume laid out before you. You didn't leave anything out, did you? Were you thinking, "That was too long ago to mention," or, "That class I took in CPR isn't important," or, "Who would care that I ran in the Chicago Marathon?" It may never make it to your final resume, but at this point, don't cast judgment. Because ya never know.

You're also not worrying about *where* you're putting the information or *how* you'll write it. That comes later. Now you're just gathering facts. You'll cut and paste later.

SUMMARY

Patience is a very handy virtue at this point. Even though you're raring to go, don't write anything yet. You need to gather ingredients. Some of it you'll use, some of it you won't. So for now, write out the facts that will illustrate your ability to do the job:

- Your strengths
- Examples of how you've used your strengths effectively
- Where you've worked and years
- Brief definition of companies you've worked for
- Your titles
- Summary of your experience
- Everything you know about
- Degrees and continuing education
- Memberships in professional groups
- Activities you're involved in
- Awards you've received
- Languages you speak
- How others describe you

chapter three

Getting to the Guts: How to Describe What You Want

Remember when you were back in high school or college and your English teacher told you to write a term paper or essay on the sociological impact of pacifism and nonviolent movements on the world or some other stimulating topic?

The first thing you had to do was come up with a thesis statement. In case you've forgotten, that was the sentence that established your stance, point of view or position on the subject. It was something like the following:

Mahatma Gandhi's campaign of nonviolence led to India's eventual independence and the illegal discrimination against the Untouchables.

Or if your paper concentrated on events closer to home, perhaps yours went like this:

Martin Luther King's followers who boycotted the Birmingham, Alabama, bus service in 1955 forced the company to change its segregated seating, and the boycott was one of the first events that impacted the Civil Rights movement.

Then, the rest of your paper had to support your point of view. Remember that?

Did you ever try to get away with not writing that thesis statement? Your paper probably reflected it. (Or maybe the grade did.) You just can't do it. If you're going to write an essay that proves a point, you have to start off by making one.

This is a good way to look at your resume. If you want prospective employers to see you in a certain light, if you want to establish yourself in their minds in a particular way, you need to establish who you are and what you can do.

Just like your term paper, your resume needs a "thesis" statement. You must figure out what you want your resume to say about you and what you want the reader to know after she reads it. Every single section of your resume will depend on it. But first, you have to know what "that" is.

So that's what you're going to learn how to do next. You may never type this statement on your resume exactly the way you write it here. But to create the body and guts of your resume, you need a statement that says:

Here's what I want to do and can do for a company, and here's how I'll make a difference.

(Don't freak out if you don't know what you want to do. I cover that in this chapter.)

By the way, this statement or a version of it can become your objective that does eventually go on your resume. More on that later too.

For now, we're developing this statement for one reason: to help you figure out what goes on or gets left off your resume. You see, once you have this sentence figured out, the only information you'll put on your resume will be that which supports your "thesis" statement.

EXAMPLE THESIS STATEMENT

I want a position in marketing where I can create marketing and communications strategies and programs, promote products and services and write persuasive promotional copy that will enhance a company's image, visibility and sales.

Wondering how this person figured hers out? Let's walk through it step-by-step.

HOW TO WRITE YOUR "THESIS" STATEMENT

Get a piece of paper or use the exercise worksheet on page 34.

Again, here's the information you're coming up with:

Here's what I want to do and can do for a company and here's how I'll make a difference.

Let's break down the three parts of this statement.

What I Want to Do

This can cover a lot of ground. It could be as general as:

advertising
accounting
management
administrative services
new product development
preventative maintenance
production
programming
retail
sales
transportation and distribution
training
purchasing
customer service
counseling
interactive multimedia

Or as specific as:

an executive producer position in broadcasting
secretary
bookkeeper
career counselor
podiatrist
management position in retail operations
construction management

What I Can Do

These are, literally, the things you can do for a company. They are your strengths, which you defined in chapter two. So here is where you list things like:

Write promotional copy
Organize and plan meetings
Coordinate schedules
Manage daily operations
Negotiate contracts
Train adults
Analyze financial data
Research marketing data
Research state-of-the-art technology
Write technical manuals
Visualize how materials and machines interface
Install and maintain software
Act as liaison between end users and programmers

How I Will Make a Difference

This is the toughie. But important as all get out. You're coming up with a sentence that explains how having you around the office all day is going to make the company better. It's not about *what* you'll do (you explained that in "What I Can Do"). It's the *result* you'll achieve.

This is hard to come up with because (1) most people don't view their work in this light and (2) once you do, it's still hard to put into words.

Please see the chart on the following page for examples of how some people made a difference in their companies.

My examples will help get you thinking. Here are some reasons why a company thought it was worth having these people around the office all day:

- Muriel, a customer service representative, *enhances customer relations.*
- Gerry, a marketing representative, *promotes the value of the company's product.*
- Erin, a manager of a retail store, *keeps operations running smoothly.*
- Diana, who worked in the transportation department of a manufacturer, *ensures the timely delivery of the company's products.*
- Lori, an administrative assistant, *ensures the efficient daily operations of her office.*
- Lois, a sales representative, *increases sales by developing new sales territories.*
- Dora, a customer service representative, *ensures good customer relations.*
- Mark, a director of support services for a school district, *contributes to the efficiency of daily operations while reducing costs and maintaining quality.*
- Morton, a controller, *contributes to the profitable growth of his company.*
- Butch, an accountant, *maintains accurate accounting records.*
- Cheryl, an executive, *strengthens the financial condition on her business.*
- Neal, an accountant, *contributes to the sound and orderly financial operation of the business.*
- Karen, a supervisor in a plant, *assures maximum equipment productivity.*
- Marlin, a supervisor, *improves productivity and enhances morale.*
- Howard, a corporate trainer, *increases staff's product knowledge that directly impacts sales.*

See what I mean? It's not a lengthy, detailed paragraph. It's a phrase that justifies your existence.

Now, let's put all three parts together so you can see the kind of statement you end up with. We'll look at Shana who is in marketing.

WHAT SHE WANTS TO DO:

Marketing communications

WHAT SHE CAN DO:

Create marketing and communications strategies and programs
Promote products and services
Write persuasive promotional copy
Work well with management and staff

HOW SHE'LL MAKE A DIFFERENCE:

Will enhance a company's image, visibility and sales

ALL TOGETHER NOW

If we put all three points together, here's the same sample thesis statement I gave before:

I want a position in marketing where I can create marketing and communications strategies and programs, promote products and services and write persuasive promotional copy that will enhance a company's image, visibility and sales.

After you develop yours, put this statement in a place where you can see it. Paste it on the wall in front of you. You'll use this to guide you through the rest of this resume-writing process.

Don't confuse this with the statement you wrote in chapter one that described *what you want your resume to do.* That was your "positioning" statement—how you want employers to perceive you.

THE "WHAT IF I DON'T KNOW WHAT I WANT TO DO?" DILEMMA

It's tougher to write this thesis statement if you don't have the slightest idea of what you want to do and how you'll make a difference. But not impossible.

Concentrate on the second part of the statement: *what I can do.* If you did the exercise in chapter two in which you identified your strengths, you know this. Right? You did do that exercise, didn't you?

Now take that information—your strengths—and write a statement like Tiffany's:

I want a position where I can use my strengths to teach concepts and ideas, communicate with enthusiasm, quickly develop rapport and facilitate mutual understanding between diverse groups of people.

Exercise: Writing Your Thesis Statement

1. What I want to do

_____
_____
_____
_____
_____
_____
_____
_____
_____

2. What I can do

_____
_____
_____
_____
_____
_____
_____
_____
_____

3. How I will make a difference

_____
_____
_____
_____
_____
_____
_____
_____

4. My thesis statement

_____
_____
_____
_____
_____
_____
_____

THE REST FOLLOWS

I know that took a lot of work. But the rest of your resume will depend on it. Plus, it makes the process of writing your resume so much easier. You'll also end up with a much better resume. When you're trying to figure out what to include in the various sections, whether to list something or leave it out, you'll look up at the wall or wherever you've strategically placed your "thesis" statement and ask, "Does this information support my thesis statement?"

EXAMPLE ONE

Barbara's thesis statement is:

I want a position in marketing where I can coordinate and execute projects, create marketing programs, organize special events and inspire others to meet goals and objectives that will build on my knowledge of the senior citizen market and result in building long-lasting relationships.

Let's say she's writing the "Experience" section of her resume (I go into detail on this in chapter five). She's wondering: "What should I include in the description of my past job experience? What about that brief stint I had when, as part of my training, I was a bank teller? Should I put that in?"

It's not going to *hurt* to include that in the description. But on the other hand, she did five other things in this job that directly *support* her statement. She:

- Planned open houses
- Coordinated educational seminars
- Organized and managed volunteers to help with special events
- Cultivated relationships with members of a special senior citizen checking account and lifestyle program
- Developed marketing programs for a senior citizen lifestyle program

These responsibilities show that she's had similar experience. The teller responsibility waters it down. So if she asked my opinion—which she did—I suggested she leave it out. (See page 103 for her completed resume, which, by the way, was responsible for getting her several interviews within two weeks and led to her next job.)

But are you still wondering one or more of the following:

1. Wouldn't she be leaving something off if she doesn't list her bank teller experience?

2. Don't you think she's not being totally truthful?

3. Don't you think that little tidbit about her being a teller might have been important or inspired the reader to think, "Gosh, she worked her way up," or "She really knows the banking business from the ground up"?

My response:

1. Yes, she's leaving something off. But so what? Your resume is supposed to be a well-organized, succinct document that covers the *relevant* information.

2. She's not in a courtroom with her hand on a Bible, swearing to tell the truth, the whole truth and nothing but the truth. She's certainly not lying. When writing a resume, you give information that is relevant and answers the interviewer's four questions we discussed in chapter one: What can you do? Have you done it and stuck with it? What do you know? What kind of person are you? This is a marketing document. It's not the place to list every boring detail of every job you had and every single course you took in your life.

3. You're trying to second-guess your audience. Everyone will see this information differently, depending on their point of view. If you spend your time trying to predict how someone might react, you'll end up with a weak mishmash of information. Remember back in chapter one when we talked about things people waste time worrying about? This was one of them.

If you like to worry, there are so many other things in life you can stew about. Like whether you remembered to give your dog its heartworm pill this month or if you sent your mother-in-law a birthday card.

When it comes to your resume, instead, concentrate on what you want your reader to know: your thesis statement and information that supports it.

Here's another example of how your thesis statement will help you when deciding what to put on your resume.

EXAMPLE TWO

Lisa only had about three years of experience since college. She wasn't sure whether to list several secretarial positions she held in college. They had nothing to do with her immediate career goal, which was to work for a larger publishing company. But they did say something else about her.

One position was at The Procter & Gamble Company. The other was in a large, reputable law firm. This experience showed that she had worked for large, conservative companies and had exposure to how these types of organizations operate. It also says that she didn't just lie around at the pool or sleep until noon during summer break. Instead, she held responsible jobs and helped pay her way through college.

If you ask me, I think this information *supports* her immediate career goal. It sure doesn't detract from it. She agreed and decided to keep this on her resume with a heading within her experience called "College Employment."

YOUR OBJECTIVE

Here's another nice thing about your thesis statement. Now you can easily turn it into your objective that would go at the top of your resume.

You've probably heard pros and cons about objectives. I lean toward putting objective statements on resumes—but *not always*. Remember, there are no rules that fit everyone and every situation. They can be advantageous if you're very focused, as in Barbara's case. (Some of the resumes in chapter eight will point that out.)

An objective is a few words, statement or bulleted points that describe what you want to do. Some people say an objective should always state the job level, such as management, and the functional area, such as transportation. Others say no matter what, always list an objective.

This is an example of Rigid Resume Syndrome (RRS), which I discussed in chapter one. I say relax. Nothing is set in stone when it comes to resumes.

As I said, I like objective statements. But if it doesn't fit you, don't use it. If you decide to use an objective, go to your thesis statement for content.

I'm also pretty loose about what an objective can look like—for the same reason I am about using an objective. Sure, I'd like you to have the perfect objective (I talk about that in a minute), but the exact wording of your objective will depend on what you have to work with.

An objective can be very general:

• Operations Management
• Account Executive
• Sales
• Administrative Assistant
• Real Estate Appraisal

It can be more detailed and include your skills and experience:

A position in retail management that requires operations and financial control experience and strong skills in training, marketing and problem solving.

Or:

To contribute a background in adult education and proven skills to:

• Write training programs
• Plan and implement educational programs
• Train adults

It can be a combination of a specific title or area, plus highlight your skills and experience:

Operations Management

A position in retail management that requires operations and financial control experience and strong skills in training, marketing and problem solving.

It can highlight your strengths:

A position that requires a broad range of consultative skills and abilities to:

• Work well with a diverse group of people
• Communicate ideas in a simple and clear fashion
• Mediate between conflicting parties to reach resolution

(Not bad, if that's all you have to work with.)

It can focus on the result you'll bring, plus touch on your experience:

To contribute to the profitable growth of an organization in a leadership position in the areas of financial planning, analysis and financial systems and operations.

ALTERNATIVES TO OBJECTIVES

If you do use an objective, I'd be pleased as punch if you could include a summary of your strengths, a reference to the type of position you want and the result you'll bring. But don't get all bent out of shape if you can't.

What if you took a ten-year hiatus from the job market? You might still be exploring what you want to do now. What if you're making a career change and don't know where you're headed? Even if you just graduated from school, you may not know where you fit in.

If that's the case with you, you'll probably develop more of a *networking resume* anyway (sample in chapter eight). This is a resume you use in informational meetings (I discussed this in chapter one) where people share ideas on what types of jobs sound appealing or can use your skills and background, which, hopefully, will help you focus on a direction. When you have a clearer picture, you can always rewrite your objective.

A networking resume may either have no objective or one that's less specific, since you may not be sure of what you want to do. Other than that, it's the same as a resume you would develop for job interviews.

If you *are* just exploring (you're conducting informational meetings) or aren't sure how to describe the position you want, your objective can focus on your skills. Or you may not even use an objective. You might use a summary statement, an overview or a profile or come up with your own heading. (Chapter four covers these kinds of options.)

Don't make a decision yet about whether or not you'll have an objective. Wait until you have all your ingredients laid out and you learn more about how you can organize them.

Crummy Objectives

- A challenging position in a growing company.
- A position that provides career development and uses my skills.
- To secure an upwardly mobile position in a progressive company where my marketing and other varied office skills can be of most benefit to an employer.

What's wrong with them?

1. They all have one thing in common: a "What you can do for me" attitude.

A company does not give you a job so you'll be challenged—that may be part of what *you* want.

A company does not hire you to provide career development—that may be what *you* had in mind.

A company does not hire you to give you security, promotions or raises—even though *you* were hoping for it.

Yet all three of these objectives convey the things *you* want—which will not win any points with employers. They are interested in what you can do for *them*.

2. None of these objectives say a darn thing. Do any of them show the reader you know who you are or what you want to do? Do any of them tell her how you'll make a difference?

This is where I get tough. If you can't write an objective that says something, don't write one. At the very least, you can figure out what your skills are, that is, what you can do. But skip all that jazz about security, challenge and being upwardly mobile. You'll annoy employers or put them out like a light.

The Good, the Bad and the Ugly About Job Titles

If you know you want to be a rocket scientist and that's the only possible title the world would call what you want to be, use a job title.

Most jobs, though, are called a variety of things. The title will depend on the company and the industry.

Also a mere title doesn't tell the reader all those wonderful things you want him to know about you.

For example, I know a woman who, if she was sitting around with a bunch of her cronies, would call herself a toxicologist. It would be OK to use that as her objective on her resume. But it would be a lot more meaningful to expand on that. This woman was smart when it came to writing her resume. Her objective reads:

OBJECTIVE

A management position in the health and environmental field or toxicology utilizing safety and regulatory experience and requiring proven abilities in project management, problem solving, research and leadership.

Doesn't that give you more information about her? I'll say. And don't you get the feeling she knows what she wants and what she has to offer?

You may limit yourself if you use a job title. The title may be too narrow. This is especially true if the functions of the job are different due to changes in the industry.

The health care industry is a perfect example. Let's say you call yourself a dietitian. That's what your training is in, and you've worked in a hospital as a dietitian for the last ten years.

Well, first of all, if you're trying to find the same kind of job that dietitians have traditionally held—in a hospital—you severely limit your opportunities.

Today, most people with this kind of experience or education are not finding the majority of jobs in hospitals. They're all over the place. Some work at schools in food service management. They operate elderly feeding programs, work at corporate cafeterias or nursing homes. They manage research projects at medical centers. They work for food pantries or magazines where they develop recipes. They teach nutrition and sanitation to people who handle food products.

So a dietitian who wants to market herself to a variety of organizations would be much more effective if she writes an objective like this:

OBJECTIVE

A position that utilizes knowledge in nutrition, food preparation and diet modification as well as proven skills to train others, research data and design and present educational programs.

And what if you're researching your next career or job and don't know what the world calls the kind of job you want? Then you definitely can't use a title.

Sneak Preview

I know you're dying to see how this thesis (which can turn into an objective) fits into the whole resume. So below is an example of how Jeremy turned his thesis into an objective, which appears at the top of his resume.

JEREMY JUSTIN
4242 Willow Place
Key West, Florida 33042
(305) 295-2020

OBJECTIVE

Position that requires an articulate communicator to enhance an organization's image and visibility and promote products or services by using strengths to:

- Clearly communicate ideas and concepts
- Plan educational activities
- Analyze sales and marketing programs
- Establish long-term customer relationships

SUMMARY

If you're serious about getting the job you want, you have to be able to describe what that is. The stronger your resume states that, the closer you will be to getting it.

Start by writing your "thesis" statement, a sentence that describes what you want to do, can do and how you'll make a difference. This statement can also be used as the objective on your resume.

When you do this up-front work, you'll also simplify the writing of your resume and end up with a dynamic marketing tool. Once you've got this statement, post it on the wall. As you're deciding whether to include something in the various sections, ask yourself, Does this information support my thesis statement or objective?

This technique also helps you focus, and, when you're nose to nose with an employer, to communicate what you want to do and how you can have an impact on a business. Hey, you didn't know a book on resumes could also help you be great in interviews, did you?

chapter four

Where You Put All This Stuff

By now you've picked up on the fact that there isn't a clear-cut, scientific, dead right way to write a resume. The same goes for how you organize it.

Life in general, and resume writing in particular, is a series of choices. Let's talk about choices when it comes to your resume. (There are just too darn many to get into when it comes to life in general.)

ALL THE HOOPLA ABOUT "FORMAT"

People like to use two basic structures: chronological and functional. I only mention these because you've probably heard of them, and if I don't bring them up, you'll think, "Well, why hasn't she brought up the most basic thing about resumes. What kind of resume expert is she anyway?"

Actually, I don't think format is the most basic—let alone the most important—thing about resumes. I do believe strongly that I don't want you to feel you have to choose one format over the other. Instead, I want you to concentrate on creating a resume that positions you to get the job you want. This may not fit into a chronological *or* functional format. It may be a combination of the two or something else.

But if you're someone who likes structure, feel free to categorize your resume any way you want. Just don't let it inhibit you from achieving what you

set out to do in chapter one (see your positioning statement). And if you didn't read the introduction to this book or forgot the third thing people waste time worrying about, from chapter one, go back and please review those now.

I'm not promoting a free-for-all. I am urging you to start out with a vision of what you want your resume to communicate. It will fit into some kind of format. But the format is a guide, not a dictator.

For the record, a *chronological resume* is just what is sounds like. It focuses on the jobs you've had and when you had them or when you went to school.

Some resume experts love chronological resumes, claim they are the most commonly used type (you do see a lot of them) and that employers prefer them. They are very straightforward and emphasize a stable work history.

Other resume experts dislike them. They think you can be more easily screened out because the emphasis is on your age, when you had your experience or how much experience you have. If any or all of those things are not in your favor, you're out of luck.

Functional resumes, also referred to as skills resumes, focus on abilities. They're organized by your skills or functions you know how to perform. They emphasize your accomplishments—not *when* you achieved them.

Some resume experts dislike functional resumes

but concede that it's the second most popular format. They're afraid employers think you're trying to disguise something such as your age, gaps between jobs or that you jumped around a lot.

Functional resumes—or versions of them—can be a good choice when you're making a career change, you have a lot of unpaid experience, your experience is varied or complicated or your actual jobs don't illustrate your abilities. You're still going to include a chronological listing of your work history.

One employer told me the type of resume she likes to see depends on the level of the employee. The more senior, the more she wants to see a big-picture thinker and someone who's results oriented. So she looks for evidence of how someone made a difference in the organizations where they worked.

Most employers tell me they don't care what you call it, they just want more than a chronological listing of your jobs. They want examples of what you've accomplished in your jobs or in your other experience.

Whew. What did all that tell you? Well sure, you can consider what someone may conclude by the format you use. But it just goes to show what I said in chapter one: You can't please everyone. Each person will have his own viewpoint and prejudices.

Incidentally, there are more than these two types of resumes. You can develop curriculum vitae or a totally creative format. But that will only get confusing and take you away from the whole point of this book—which is to create a resume that helps you achieve your goal of getting the job you want, not one that fits a format.

Samples of the two most common formats follow on pages 41-43. But from this point on, you'll rarely hear me refer to any of my sample resumes as either chronological or functional because I simply don't create resumes based on format. Why does it matter what format it is? Who cares? The resumes I include in this book are a combination of formats that my clients and I decided best marketed them for the positions they wanted. Isn't that what you're trying to accomplish?

Binders and Other Overkill

Occasionally someone asks me whether they should put their resume in a binder. No, I tell them. "But don't you think it looks really professional?"

they insist. No, I tell them. "Isn't it more substantial?" they continue. Your resume should stand on its own, I tell them, "Won't I stand out more in a binder?" they go on. Stand out with a great resume, is my response.

Besides, most employers file resumes. Binders make that hard to do. If your resume is a couple pages, just send it as is, with your name on each page (no staples, please).

One man sent me a six-page resume in a binder that listed every program and workshop he was involved in and course he took. Awful, isn't it? The appropriateness of a binder wasn't even the question. He just sent way too much information.

I've also seen people send copies of every article they've written or been quoted in with copies of their resumes. Unless someone requests it, just send your resume and a cover letter. *Capisce?*

RESUME SECTIONS

You've already written the content for most of these sections in chapter two. (Remember all the "ingredients" you wrote?) As you read through each section, I've noted where you can go back and find this content. The only information you haven't already written out is for these first three sections: name, address and phone number.

Your Name

Use your full name:

Patrick R. Manilla

Don't list yourself like this:

Patrick "Ricky" Manilla

Or:

William "Bucky" Masters (even if that's what your friends call you)

You don't have to use a middle initial. And I shy away from using middle names. They seem cumbersome on a resume.

Your Address

Spell out your street address, city and state:

1598 Medford Road
Columbus, Ohio 43209

Example of chronological format

MITCHELL PING
444 East Nordic Way
Boston, Massachusetts 02117
(617) 447-2121

OBJECTIVE

Compensation and benefit management

EXPERIENCE

1985-Present
Dugan & Daughters, Boston, Massachusetts
<u>Vice President, Compensation and Benefits</u>
Oversee wage and salary program and benefits for 2,500 employees of national retail chain. Analyze and develop job descriptions and administer performance evaluations.

1980-1985
Lucas, Luke and Lake, Austin, Texas
<u>Director, Compensation</u>
Designed and implemented wage and salary programs and record keeping system for 200 employees of law firm. Wrote employment practices and policies and developed job descriptions and evaluation process. Handled administration of fringe benefits and insurance.

1975-1980
Frankly, Frank and Frugal, Princeton, New Jersey
<u>Compensation Analyst</u>
Analyzed salary and benefits data for 150 employees of accounting firm. Developed computerized reports and implemented automated employee data system. Conducted research.

EDUCATION

M.B.A.
Butler College 1985

Bachelor of Arts in Business Administration
University of New Hampshire 1975

MEMBERSHIPS

National Association of Compensation Professionals
Benefits Managers of America
Personnel Manager Professionals

Example of functional format

LOUIE LOUIE
11 Pixie Way
Santa Cruz, California 95066
(408) 477-8080

OBJECTIVE

Position that will utilize a broad range of consulting skills, knowledge in financial planning and analysis, accounting and training and strengths to:
- Analyze complex financial data
- Quickly develop rapport and build trusting relationships
- Work effectively with diverse types of people
- Mediate between conflicting parties to explore options and reach resolution

SUMMARY OF QUALIFICATIONS

Seventeen years' experience in training, financial planning and consulting and accounting for small businesses. Known for ability to translate complex financial data into understandable information and develop sound financial plans for individuals and small businesses. Knowledge includes:
- Accounting management
- Small business management
- Business plans and projections
- Corporate and individual tax planning
- Retirement planning, investment, risk management
- Thorough understanding of health insurance and regulatory compliance

EXPERIENCE

FINANCIAL PLANNING AND ACCOUNTING:

Financial Planning Consultant
Lexerol Company, Los Angeles, California   1990-1995
Consulted with small businesses to meet financial goals, develop business plans and internal control procedures for financial firm managing over $100 million in assets.
- Acted as liaison between owner of company and buyer that included the development of compensation package for former owner and resulted in smooth transfer of ownership.
- Assessed tax ramifications for business that was considering investment in foreign market; saved company from potential $2 million loss.

Financial Planner

Howard & Howard, Inc., San Francisco, California   1984-1989

Managed $55 million in portfolio assets for small business clients and individuals. Wrote financial plans. Trained and managed administrative staff. Handled documentation to assure regulatory compliance. Traded securities.

• Acted as mediator between families and business owners whose financial philosophies differed, leading to mutual understanding and meeting of goals.

Staff Accountant

Big Big Eight Firm, San Francisco, California   1982-1984

Oversaw small business audits and prepared individual income tax returns. Compiled financial statements for partnerships and trusts.

TRAINING:

Instructor

Burton School of Business, San Francisco, California   1980-1984

Taught financial planning for Adult Education Division. Created curriculum and training materials.

• Rated Best Instructor three consecutive years.

Instructor

Mitsubini Electronics, San Francisco, California   1995-1997

Conducted six-week training courses of personal financial planning for union workers at major electronic parts manufacturer.

EDUCATION

Master of Business Administration Lundy School of Management
University of Texas 1981

B.S. in Accounting University of Texas 1980

Certified Financial Planner Designation
Licenses include: Series 63, 65, Life, Health and Variable Annuity Insurance

82 West 82 Street
Apartment B-11
New York, New York 10023

Your Phone Number

Put the area code and your home phone number. You may also want to include an office phone number and e-mail address. Be sure to designate what each number is.

Some people say you should never put an office phone number on your resume because it sends a nasty message: You're looking for another job on your present employer's time. That is true. Maybe. It depends how you're using the phone number.

If you're holding lengthy conversations with potential future employers, you cross into dangerous territory. On the other hand, when an employer calls, you can say something like: "I'm glad you were able to reach me during the day; otherwise we'd probably be playing phone tag. Would it be OK if we set a time to talk further after my workday?"

This approach does two things: (1) makes it more convenient for the employer to reach you and (2) demonstrates your commitment to your present employer.

Nowadays, some business phone numbers listed on resumes are outplacement offices where people conduct their job searches.

The other issue to consider is this: You probably want to keep the lid on the fact that you're looking for a job. Getting calls at work from prospective employers can blow your cover. Someone could see a phone message or overhear your conversation.

If you're worried about it for any reason, don't include an office phone number. But get an answering machine or voice mail at home so employers can leave messages. And return calls promptly.

Your Objective

This tells what you want to do, and, as I said in chapter three, possibly a summary of your strengths and the result you'll bring. *Pleeeaase* read the section on objectives (pages 36-38) to decide how detailed yours will get, or if you'll even use one.

Optional Beginnings (Instead of an Objective)

Use the word *Summary* or *Profile*.

You can find the content for this in the lists you developed of:

- Your strengths
- Your expertise in a nutshell
- Whaddaya know?
- How the world sees you

Examples:

SUMMARY *— Your expertise in a nutshell*
(Health care executive with 15 years in a teaching hospital. Background includes administrative responsibility for clinical operations including pathology, rehabilitation, ambulatory care and medical records.) *— Whaddaya know?*
(Extensive experience in risk management and quality assurance. Strong patient care orientation.)

PROFILE *— Your expertise in a nutshell*
(An experienced sales and marketing professional with a successful track record developing new business and strategic business plans in the retail shoe industry.) (Reputation for getting results under demanding deadlines.) *— How the world sees you* *Your expertise in a nutshell*
(Executive with extensive knowledge in broadcasting and proven history of success in leading organizations through change.) *— Your strengths*
(Superior skills in strategic planning, communications, building consensus and achieving bottom-line results through people.) (Expertise in operations, marketing and sales. Keen understanding of industry trends.) *— Whaddaya know?*

Qualifications or Summary of Qualifications

This is a summary of why you're qualified to do what you want and/or an overview of your career and your expertise. This is where you can list other languages you speak and hardware and software knowledge. You can draw from what you wrote in five places in chapter two:

- Your strengths
- Your expertise in a nutshell

- Whaddaya know?
- Habla Español?
- How the world sees you

Look at the following examples to see how you can combine information.

EXAMPLES OF QUALIFICATIONS

How the world sees you ↙

(A mature, goal-oriented problem solver) (with four years' educational and hands-on experience working with culturally diverse groups of people in nonprofit and business settings.) Areas of knowledge include: *Your expertise in a nutshell*

- Volunteer recruitment   *Whaddaya know?*
- Training
- Fund-raising
- Market research
- Special event planning
- Budgets
- Fluency in Spanish ← *Habla Español?*

SUMMARY OF QUALIFICATIONS

How the world sees you ↘   *Your expertise in a nutshell*

(A diplomatic, efficient-minded service technician) (with seven years in supervision and repair and maintenance of buildings, equipment and electrical and operational systems.) (Reputation for being resourceful and staying coolheaded in emergencies.) Expertise includes:

How the world sees you or your strengths

- HVAC systems
- Preventative maintenance
- Inventory control   ← *Whaddaya know?*
- Purchasing
- Remodeling skills, including roofing, masonry, woodworking, dry wall, plumbing

Accomplishments

These are brief, concise statements that illustrate your strengths or areas of expertise.

For example, if you stated in your objective or summary at the beginning of your resume that you had a track record in developing new business, here's where you prove it. If you said you were an accomplished trainer, this is where you give a hard-hitting example.

You wrote the content for this in chapter two under "Proof." Now rewrite these examples so that

they start with a verb and describe what you did and the result. So that means, if you didn't already, you need to quantify your efforts.

"But . . . I don't know how my work affected the company. . . . I got laid off before the program was instituted. . . . I don't have access to that information. . . . My job isn't quantifiable." Any of those thoughts going through your head?

This information may not be easy for you to come up with. It may not be possible to quantify something you did. But think about whether you can get your hands on this data before you start yelling at me. And take a look at the difference between the weak and the stronger version of each accomplishment I've listed on page 46. The stronger one always quantifies the result. It hits employers smack-dab where it matters to them—in the pocket.

If you absolutely, positively can't show how you had impact on the bottom line by giving specific cost savings or percentages, the next best thing is to use adjectives that describe the result.

EXAMPLES:

- Developed process for reengineering 200-person division that *significantly cut costs.*
- Developed new training for customer service staff that *dramatically enhanced customer service and morale.*

Sometimes your results aren't easily measured in numbers.

EXAMPLES:

- Conducted research for nonprofit organization that led to public support of historic renovation and saved four historical sites in New York.
- Developed training materials for health care organization that cross trained over 60 employees.
- Recruited 25 volunteers for nonprofit organization that increased community awareness of group.
- Mediated between dozens of families that led to mutual understanding and meeting of financial goals.
- Created and implemented public relations campaign that significantly improved perception of company in marketplace.

If you're a recent graduate, use your community

EXAMPLES OF WEAK AND STRONGER ACCOMPLISHMENT STATEMENTS

Weak:
Initiated process that reduced production costs at manufacturing plant, saving company money.

Stronger:
Initiated process that reduced production costs at manufacturing plant saving company $8,500 annually.

Weak:
Repaired outdated boiler system from 1930s that saved company costly new heating system.

Stronger:
Repaired outdated boiler system from 1930s that saved company $40,000 for new heating system.

Weak:
Strategically planned and marketed state-of-the-art recording studio that generates yearly revenue and has successfully competed for market share.

Stronger:
Strategically planned and marketed state-of-the-art recording studio that generates $350,000 in yearly revenue and has successfully competed for 30% of market share.

Weak:
Developed process for reengineering 200-person division that cut costs.

Stronger:
Developed process for reengineering 200-person division that saved $5.2 million annually.

Weak:
Converted manual accounting system for retail company into integrated system that helped company build its business.

Stronger:
Converted manual accounting system for retail company into integrated system that tripled business volume in first year.

---

involvement, school projects or other work experience such as the third example above.

Sometimes getting so specific isn't a good idea if it can damage an employer. So be careful you don't share proprietary information or confidential facts and figures. Either find a way to be more general or use a different example.

These accomplishments can go into their own section on your resume called "Accomplishments" or "Achievements." Or they can be listed as bullet points *within* your experience.

One of my clients told me she was sold on listing hers within her experience since employers tended to jump to her experience and ask questions.

This also helps the reader know where your accomplishments occurred. If you do list them in a separate section, you can indicate where they happened so the reader doesn't have to guess. For example, say:

- Repaired outdated boiler system from 1930s that heated 250 apartments, saving management firm $40,000 for new heating system.

The reader can go to your experience to see when you worked for an apartment complex with 250 units.

When trying to decide which accomplishments to list, look back at your thesis statement developed in chapter three and strengths you listed in chapter two. What are you trying to prove? Give examples to support that.

Experience

This is a listing of your jobs, starting with your most recent position. Include company name, city and state, division you worked for, your titles, brief definition of the company, dates (years only) and a brief description of what you did.

If you're wondering whether to list jobs you had in college or ones you held fifteen to twenty years ago, first look at your thesis statement. Does the information you're wondering whether to include support it? Second, are the jobs so long ago, they're irrelevant? You wrote the information for this section in chapter two under:

- Where you worked and when
- What in the world do they do?

• What do they call you, and what do you do all day?

Here's how this section might look when you put all those points together:

Where you worked

WNCR Radio, Marysville, North Carolina

What did they call you? *When?* → 1987-1996

Engineering Director *What did you do all day?*

Managed engineering function for one of top public radio stations in U.S. with annual budget of over $2 million. Oversaw budget and capital expenditures for studio facilities. Supervised production facility, remote and studio recordings, technical program production and uplink satellite distribution. Managed recording engineer and audio and satellite assistants.

Education

List your highest degree first, the institution you graduated from and the year and other continuing or relevant education. You wrote this information in chapter two under "Are You Educated?"

New graduates can put the degree at the beginning of the resume in a section such as "Qualifications." (See chapter eight for examples.) If your grades are good, list your grade point average. If not, don't list it.

EXAMPLES OF HOW THIS WILL LOOK:

Bachelor of Arts Journalism
University of North Carolina 1984
Master in Health Services Administration with concentration in long-term care
Xavier University 1990 GPA 3.78

Professional Affiliations

These are professional and trade organizations you belong to and you listed in chapter two under "Do You Belong to Professional Groups?"

Community Interests or Activities

List the groups and community activities you participate in and any offices you've held. You wrote this in chapter two under "Are You a Joiner?"

If you decide to list information like your involvement in the Chicago Marathon or anything else that doesn't seem to fit under professional memberships or another category, this is a good spot for it.

Awards

Write awards and recognition you've received and you wrote under "Oscars and Other Recognition." These can also be listed as achievements in a section called "Achievements," as bullet points within your experience or in a section at the end of your resume called "Awards."

SILLY THINGS PEOPLE INCLUDE
The Phrase "References Available Upon Request"

Now what does that mean? That if the person reading your resume wants your references, he can ask. Duh. Did you need to tell him that? Everybody knows that. The only reason you put that on *your* resume is because you see it on everyone *else's* resume. So you figure it's supposed to be there. Why take up room with a meaningless statement that everybody already knows?

You might ask, "Just when do I bring up my references?" When somebody asks for them.

Supervisors', Managers' and Colleagues' Names

There are several reasons not to include these:

1. Remember back in chapter one when I talked about recruiters and what they do with your resume? Well, besides looking for information about what kind of technology a particular company is using, they may also use your resume to find job candidates for their clients. If you list the person you work for or people you work with, you may be weakening *your* chances to be considered. Besides, you're not working for the recruiter.

2. What do the people you worked for or with have to do with the goal you're trying to achieve with this resume (which is to hook and hold someone's attention and show them how *you* can improve their life)? You got it. Nothing.

A Photograph

What you look like has nothing to do with whether you're qualified for the job you're applying for. So don't give employers irrelevant information. Some employers may use what you look like (race, sex or some aspect of your face that they decide they don't like) as a reason to discriminate against

Resume Sections

SECTION	WHAT IT TELLS EMPLOYERS	HOW IMPORTANT IS IT?
NAME, ADDRESS AND PHONE	• Who you are and how to reach you	Extremely
OBJECTIVE	• What you want to do and if it matches position that's open	Very, but not compulsory
QUALIFICATIONS	• An overview of your career and why you're qualified for the job you want • Whether you have the kind of expertise needed; whether you're the kind of person they want *(What can you do? What do you know? What kind of person are you?)	Very, but not compulsory
ACCOMPLISHMENTS	• Specific ways you've been successful in your life and past jobs • How you can help the employer *(What can you do?)	Extremely
EXPERIENCE	• The kinds of jobs you've had, progression, responsibility, types of organizations you've worked for *(What can you do? Have you done it and stuck with it?)	Extremely
EDUCATION	• What type of training you have and if it's applicable to the job *(What do you know?)	Depends on job; can be mandatory
PROFESSIONAL AFFILIATIONS	• How committed you are to your professional growth	Can't hurt
COMMUNITY INTERESTS OR ACTIVITIES	• Your hobbies and interests outside of work • Shows balance and interest in others *(What kind of person are you?)	Nice to have; could be important to some employers
AWARDS	• If you've done outstanding work and been recognized by your peers	Nice to have

*Refers to the four things most everyone wants to know: (1) What can you do? (2) Have you done it and stuck with it? (3) What do you know? and (4) What kind of person are you?

you. But this would be tough to prove. So don't give them the chance.

Obviously, this wisdom does not apply to someone who makes their living by what they look like (a model or other kind of talent).

"Salary Negotiable" or Any Mention of Salary in Past Positions

Salary is irrelevant at this point. You haven't been offered a position. So why bring it up? By listing what you want or made in the past you:

- Potentially screen yourself out of the running—if you want megabucks or, on the other hand, too low of a salary
- Weaken your ability to negotiate later—because the employer knows what you want or were making

Besides all that, what you made at other jobs has nothing to do with your next one.

Mention of Being Disabled

A woman who used a wheelchair told me that it helped if she let employers know in advance that she was disabled. This put them at ease because they weren't surprised and had taken care of the necessary accommodations. But she only shared this information *after* she got the interview. So don't put it on your resume or cover letter.

HOW TO PICK AND CHOOSE

Should you use an "Objective" or a "Summary" or "Profile" section at the beginning of your resume? Look at what you've got to work with. If you have a strong objective and it explains what you're looking for, use it. If the summary approach looks like it captures you better in a nutshell, use that. I'm giving you options and letting you be judge based on your career objective, work history and personal circumstances.

Do you list jobs you had in college? First, that depends on how long ago college was. Second, it depends on whether it's relevant to your current career objective. If you've been a professional for awhile (five or more years), you probably have more current experience to support your thesis state-ment. On the other hand, there may be something about that experience that supports a point you want to make loud and clear (see chapter three story of Lisa who included college experience).

You don't have to include everything you listed in chapter two. Some of it may not support your thesis statement or objective.

At this point you can decide what information you want to keep or discard and you have general or specific ideas of where you see it fitting and some of the wording you'll use. In the next chapter you can fine-tune your writing.

SUMMARY

How you structure your resume is not the most important thing. What matters is if your resume does its job. It shows employers what you know, what you've accomplished, what you can do in the future and gets them curious enough to want to know more about you.

There are some sections that are a must on a resume, including your name, address and phone, your experience and specific examples that show how you've been successful in your life and and past jobs. Format, though, is not what you need to dwell on.

You laid out all the "ingredients" for your resume in chapter two. Use the information that supports your thesis. Throw out what doesn't. Decide what to call a certain section, what to include in it and what you want to emphasize or de-emphasize because of how you want to position yourself. As you create your resume, look up at your wall where you posted your thesis statement and ask, "Am I proving that?"

chapter five

How to Write With Pizzazz

I f you—or other people—think you're the greatest thing since sliced bread, then darn it, say it on your resume.

OK, maybe the sliced bread thing is carrying it a bit far.

But your resume is the place to boast about your reputation and praise yourself on a job well done. Here's where a thesaurus comes in handy. Because you'll be looking for alluring, tantalizing, soul-stirring and galvanizing ways (I got those words from my thesaurus) to entice the reader to go on to the next word. That's good writing. And remember, your goal is to write a captivating resume.

Now I know it won't come easy to write like this. Your parents probably told you not to brag about yourself. Even Senator Bob Dole, whose whole career has been in public service, has trouble calling himself "I." Apparently he refers to himself as "Bob Dole." In Bob Woodward's book *The Choice*, he says Dole explained that he was taught not to call himself "I" because his mother considered it bragging.

To write with pizzazz, you'll also have to break some writing habits. Most of your career or school life you've probably been writing ho-hum business babble or stilted school drool. But that just won't do if you're going to get the job you want. Do you want to put the employer to sleep or inspire her? Well then, let's get on with doing the latter.

RESUMESQUE WRITING

Resumes are written in a style that's different than any other type of writing I can think of. It goes against what your second grade elementary school-teacher pounded into your head about always writing complete sentences. And you're discouraged to do what your high school creative writing teacher said about expressing feelings. Yet, you can't bore the reader with businessy-sounding memo talk.

Your goal here is to write every section with confidence, brevity, clarity and, of course, don't forget gusto. And you do it as if you're talking about a product and its benefits—the product being you—in the third person. The language should be brief and bulleted.

Use Active, Not Passive, Words

This helps you use fewer words and ones that are crisper and easier to understand. Look at the difference:

PASSIVE	ACTIVE
Responsible for creating and implementing strategies.	Created and implemented strategies.

Here are some action words to have around (come up with your own, as well):

advised	investigated
analyzed	led
arranged	managed
boosted	mediated
built	negotiated
coached	operated
constructed	organized
coordinated	oversaw
counseled	persuaded
created	pioneered
designed	planned
devised	proposed
directed	presented
drafted	published
edited	revised
expanded	researched
facilitated	spearheaded
founded	streamlined
handled	supervised
improvised	trained
inspired	transcribed
installed	wrote

FAT	TRIM
The balance of	The rest
Completed inventory on a regular basis.	Completed regular inventory.
Gave performance reviews on an annual basis.	Conducted annual performance reviews.

Eliminate Unnecessary Articles Such as *A*, *An* and *The*

Be as clear as possible, but the fewer words the better. See the difference:

• *Sentence using articles*

Created and implemented the strategies for the reengineering program.

• *Edited version*

Created and implemented strategies for reengineering program.

Don't Use *I* , *Me*, *My* or *As Programmer, I* at the Beginnings of Sentences

It's understood that you're talking about you and your career. (See chapter eight's "Yechy Resumes" section that shows you a real dilly.)

Trim the Fat

Once you write a statement, look at it and ask, "How can I simplify this? What can I cut?" For example:

This can be hard to do. You get rather attached to words you write. So you have to be tough on yourself.

I write a weekly newspaper column that takes up a full column length of space. That adds up to about 680 words. My first draft is always too long. So then I have to strap on my chopping hat and cut out unnecessary words and phrases. It's painful, but it always makes the article better in the end. It's the same with your resume.

All Verbs and Subjects Should Agree

For example, here's what one man wrote on his resume:

Planned and developed courses, training delivery and evaluation of performance.

He meant to say:

Planned and developed courses, delivered training and evaluated job performance.

Someone else wrote:

Sold and serviced trade show exhibit accounts.

She meant to say:

Sold trade show exhibits and serviced up to 10 local accounts.

(You sell exhibits, not accounts. You service accounts.)

After you write a sentence, go back to your verb and see what it describes. It takes more time but makes you look much smarter and competent when it's right.

Avoid Abbreviations and Shortcuts

These are words like *etc.*, *Co.* (if that's not part of the company's full name) and *depts.* It's OK to abbreviate states (CA, OH, MI) and degrees, such as B.A. and Ph.D.

Eliminate Jargon

This is especially important if you are looking for a job in a field different than where you've been or if your company uses "company-speak" that means nothing to anyone outside the company's walls.

Examples I found on resumes:

- Initiated analysis of facilitationable implementation of consolidation locations. (Huh?)
- Solved problems through opportunity identification and development and creation of Win-Win solutions that supported policies. (Have no idea what this means.)
- Developed proposal for major intervener in company's alternative purchasing filing. (Go figure.)

Don't Use Complete Sentences

Start statements with the active verb that describes what you did or the adjectives or adverbs that describe you. Also, phrases can stand by themselves. Examples:

COMPLETE SENTENCE	EDITED VERSION
As a senior executive, I developed knowledge in . . .	Senior executive with knowledge in . . .
I have an outstanding track record in sales. My knowledge includes industry trends.	Outstanding track record in sales. In-depth knowledge of industry trends.
Every year I organized the meeting.	Organized annual meeting.
I completed 30 credit hours that will apply toward B.A. in English.	30 credit hours toward B.A. in English.
Have been promoted while at company.	Positions of increasing responsibility.

Keep the Same Tense

What's so important about it? I'll let a human resource person tell you:

> *It's extremely annoying when tenses are used inconsistently and inappropriately. It can be confusing, it puts into question the writer's command of proper English grammar and demonstrates a lack of attention to detail.*

So there.

It's OK to describe the job you're in now with the present tense. Just make sure you describe it in the present tense in the first sentence, second sentence and the entire job description. Don't switch back and forth between tenses. Example:

Control *day-to-day operations*. Create *and* implement strategies.

Not:

Control *day-to-day operations*. Created *and* implemented *strategies*.

The same goes for previous jobs. If you start out describing a job in the past tense, make sure every sentence that describes that particular job is in the past tense. Also, if you write one previous job in the past tense, write all *other* previous jobs in the past tense.

Some people like to write all of their job descriptions (even past jobs) in the present tense. Fine with me. Just be consistent throughout every job.

The same human resource person from earlier says it's not fine with her, however. She says it can mislead a reader to think you're now responsible for tasks you haven't handled for years. (See what I mean about not being able to please everyone?)

BLEAHY WRITING

I found the phrases on the next page on various resumes that I categorize as bleahy (you say that with a "ha" sound) writing because they have one or more of the following in common:

- They don't say or mean anything.
- They aren't clear as to what they mean.
- They are vague and therefore meaningless.
- They have good intentions but use the wrong wording.

All of that is bleahy to me. To improve the bleahy version, I've had to make some assumptions as to what the writer meant. But you get the gist of it.

ADJECTIVES AND ADVERBS ADD SPICE

They can describe you, something you did or the result of your work. Keep a list handy. Here are some that I like:

analytical	highly organized
articulate	in-depth
astute	innovative
committed	mature
compassionate	passionate
conceptual	persuasive
conscientious	profitable
considerable	progressive
consistent	proven
creative	resourceful
decisive	responsible
dedicated	self-motivated
detail-minded	strategic
diplomatic	substantial
enthusiastic	swift
extensive	take-charge
fair	tenacious
focused	thorough
goal-oriented	uncompromising
hands-on	

BLEAHY	IMPROVED
Further building of staff.	Train staff on new procedures.
Proficient experience in sales.	Experienced salesperson. or Proficient in sales techniques.
Making staff assignments.	Oversee daily staff assignments.
Attending meetings.	Participate in weekly budget meetings.

BLEAHY	IMPROVED
Selling of additional services.	Sell monthly subscriptions and annual memberships.
Selling as well as selling over the telephone.	Conduct one-on-one presentations and telephone sales.
Doing daily numbers tally.	Tally daily sales.
Also heavily involved in program acquisition.	Oversee program acquisition.
Responsible for all areas of publicity.	Handle all publicity including media relations, press conferences and interviews.
Well versed in several aspects of organization.	Well organized.
Created architectural ideas for real-world clients.	Developed architectural concepts for corporate clients.

And finally, two of my favorites:

BLEAHY	IMPROVED
Constant usage of excellent communication skills.	Excellent communication skills. or Skilled communicator.

(Makes you wonder if she really is a skilled communicator using a phrase like that.)

BLEAHY	IMPROVED
Short but distinguished experience in managing.	Managed administrative staff and intern.

NO BUSINESS BABBLE OR SCHOOL DROOL

This is a mindset that businesspeople get into that they may have learned in school. It's as if they wake up in the morning, put on their suits and shift into a formal, stilted way of communicating. Here's an example from a real letter from a really big company.

I have canvassed regarding availability for the attendance of all directors at this meeting, but have not heard from those participating as of this writing.

Why not just say:

I don't have a head count yet on which directors will attend the meeting.

Or:

I don't know which directors will attend the meeting yet.

Because businesspeople write and talk like this, business babble makes its way into resumes that read like this:

OBJECTIVE

To associate with the business of music, art and entertainment in the role of management with the ultimate goal of involvement in the creative aspects of this business.

Why not just say:
Entertainment and arts management.

QUALIFICATIONS

Able to interface with other professionals regarding development of marketing strategies and market analysis.

If I get her drift, she's saying she's a team player and has expertise in market analysis and developing marketing strategies. Why not just say that?

EXPERIENCE

*Manager, VIP Company   1990-Present
Responsible for providing an environment that was proactive in supporting management in resolving conflict, maintaining audit requirements and facilitating organizational restructuring, and effective administration of the employee function for a population of 1,000 employees.*

(I hesitate to rewrite this description without clarifying what the writer meant. But you get the idea.)

OTHER TENDENCIES YOU SHOULD KILL
Too Good to Be True

Sometimes you can carry your descriptions too far and sound highfalutin or pompous. This could send up red flags that you're either too good to be true or have an ego the size of the Mississippi River. Here are some examples I found that make me squirm:

- Innate analytical prowess.
- Invaluable asset.
- Participation in academic governance has provided in-depth understanding of problems confronting today's educational institutions including information technology obsolescence.
- Trustworthiness and leadership qualities that are substantiated.

Got It Off of Someone Else's Resume (or Out of a Book)

Just because you like a phrase on someone's resume doesn't mean you can use it successfully. Before he became my client, Alan had this on his resume:

"Have developed innovative ideas into effective programs."

"What's that mean?" I asked him.

"I saw it on someone's resume and thought it sounded good," he replied.

(This is precisely the kind of question he could hear in an interview. Boy, would that look bad if he couldn't explain it.)

When he became my client, we deleted that from his resume and rewrote it so it meant something.

Here's how you can punch up a weak statement like that. If you really have been innovative, explain what you did and how if was effective:

Developed innovative marketing plan that produced enough leads for company to meet its annual sales goal in five months.

I have a client who has only been in his career a few years. He wanted to sound like he had more experience, so he pulled phrases out of a book, such as "Management expertise." When I asked him about his management expertise, he said, "Well I've worked for managers." That's not having expertise as a manager.

Whenever you write a sentence, look at it and ask yourself, "Does this really say anything? Can I explain what it means if I'm asked?" If you can't, rewrite it or get rid of it.

Don't Make Me Laugh

I'm not sure if the writer of this statement was trying to be funny or just chose the wrong words:

A sense of humor that has allowed me to simultaneously tackle several tasks and unexpected problems without losing my mind.

Either way, I'm not laughing. If I were an employer, I'd eliminate him from the running. If you're thinking about using humor on your resume, don't. It's not the place for it, and it can be misunderstood.

Sometimes people tell me they want to be creative with their resumes. Overall, I've found that resumes are best when they are straightforward and don't try to be cute or too creative. Now if you're in a creative field, you may want to create a totally different kind of resume than the type I'm talking about here. I've seen some very clever ones like the one that took the form of a record (the kind we played on our stereos before there were cassettes and CDs). That's different. And that's not a format this book will address.

A Word on Punctuation

One of my clients just cannot accept that I put periods at the end of statements that are not complete sentences. Therefore, every statement on her resume has no punctuation at the end. For example, she describes her most recent position like this:

Planned national sales meeting including development of collateral materials for sales force

I think it looks like she forgot to punctuate. But c'est la vie. Don't be afraid to end statements with periods, even if they're not complete sentences. You need to bring the reader to the end of a thought at some point.

LANGUAGE FOR THE 1990s AND BEYOND

Here are words and phrases that speak the language of today's employers. Look for ways to integrate them into your resume. Many may not apply to you, so don't force it. Just be aware that companies today are trying to respond to consumers in highly competitive domestic and international markets. Many of these words hit their hot buttons:

bottom line
team building
results-oriented
meet profit objectives
cost reductions
consolidate
cycle time
innovation
passion
safety awareness
quality
diversity
international
strategic planning
start-up
continuous improvement
streamline
PC fluent
bilingual

HOW TO MAKE COMPLICATED THINGS SOUND SIMPLE

All of the advice I've given so far about being brief and concise applies to every section of your resume, from your objective to your job descriptions. When you create your experience section, though, it can be tougher to write this way.

Here's why. If I asked you to explain what you do at your job (or want to do), could you explain it in about thirty words and so your mother understood? Well, more or less, that's what you want to do on your resume. The more detailed and complicated your work and accomplishments are, the more difficult that is.

One of my clients, Patrice, was a manager for a consumer products manufacturer. She wanted to move into a different field, so it was especially important for her to describe her past position in simple, nonjargon language. When I asked her to describe her job she wrote:

> *Responsible for multifunctional team to evaluate and recommend short/long-term trade spending strategies to integrate products including off-invoice allowances, advertising funding and combined orders.*

I don't know about you, but not being in that business, I don't have the slightest idea what she does. Here's how we got her job description into English. More or less, this is our conversation. I'm including it here so you see what you will probably need to go through yourself.

Me: I want you to tell me about one key function you perform in this job. In other words, if you could pick one single word that describes one of the main things you do, what is it?

Patrice: Well, I'm responsible for this multifunctional team. (Obviously, that wasn't one word. It's not that Patrice didn't understand the instructions. She's actually quite bright. It's just not easy to do.)

Me: So you *lead* this team.

Patrice: Yes, exactly.

So now we know that one of her key functions, which is what you're describing when you tell about your experience, is to *lead*. She can start the sentence with that verb. Now back to our conversation.

Me: Who do you lead?

Patrice: I told you, a team.

(She got a little annoyed at this point.)

Me: But who's on that team?

Patrice: Oh. Sales reps and managers.

Me: How many sales reps and managers?

Patrice: Six sales reps and two managers.

Now we know that she leads a team of six sales representatives and two managers.

Me: What do you lead them to do?

Patrice: To do their jobs.

(She was really bugged.)

Me: Which is what?

Patrice: To evaluate and recommend short- and

long-term spending strategies and integrate products into our overall ad plan. Which I told you before and you said you didn't like it.

(I still don't.)

Me: I don't know what that means. Do you develop advertising strategies?

Patrice: Yes. We also work closely with co-op advertisers.

(Now we're getting somewhere.)

So, in essence, she helps lead this team to evaluate how their division will spend advertising dollars that included co-op advertising.

So she can now rewrite her job experience like this:

> *Lead a team of six sales representatives and two managers in foot care divisions to develop advertising strategies that work in conjunction with co-op advertisers.*

Now that is English.

Do you see how easy it is to assume others know what you mean? You do your job every day. You get immersed in the jargon. The person reading your resume isn't there, though. So you have to explain it. Even if you're job hunting in the same field you're now in, explain your job in plain English.

Since I won't be there with you to write this, I'll show you how to hold this kind of conversation with yourself. Let's go through another example. This time you're in public relations.

You ask yourself: If I could pick one single word that describes one of the main things I do, what is it?

You answer: I "present" information.

You ask yourself: What kind of information do I present?

You answer: Plans, objectives, program benefits, new product lines.

You ask yourself: Whom do I present this information to? Where do I present it?

You answer: To the media, stockholders, other employees, sales staff. At press conferences and sales meetings.

Now you can put this all together to describe one key function of your job by saying that you:

Present plans, objectives, program benefits and new product lines to various audiences, including media, company stockholders and staff.

If another one of your key functions is to organize press conferences and sales meetings, you can say:

Organize and coordinate press conferences and annual sales meeting for 250 sales representatives.

Then put together all the key functions of your job. Now you can describe what used to sound very complex and confusing to an outsider in clear and simple language:

Present plans, objectives, program benefits and new product lines to various audiences, including media, company stockholders and staff. Organize and coordinate press conferences and annual sales meeting for 250 sales representatives.

You need to write your experience like this whether someone is in your industry or not. To keep your accomplishments brief and uncomplicated, use the formula I showed you in chapter four: Start with the verb that describes what you did, then give the result.

INTERESTING WAYS TO SAY BORING THINGS
Get Specific

Besides using adjectives and adverbs, jazz up your writing by giving the scope of events, including percentages and figures whenever possible.

For example, one of my clients organized a major golf tournament. When he wrote his achievement it read:

Organized annual golf tournament that raised money for the Jaycees.

Pretty boring? I'll say.

When I asked him questions, I found out the tournament attracted celebrities, gained international media and raised over $60,000. So we rewrote it to read:

Coordinated and managed three-day golf tournament that attracted such celebrities as

Jackie Gleason and Bob Hope and international media; event raised $60,000 for the Jaycees.

When you talk about your qualifications, you can also list the very specific knowledge you have that you wrote about in chapter two:

QUALIFICATIONS
Knowledge includes:
• Public speaking
• Understanding of legislative process
• Press conferences
• Working closely with lobbyists

Personalize
Don't be afraid to describe yourself the way others do (see chapter two). Some of those words distinguish you from everybody else. For example, check out how we zipped up Karen's description of herself. She initially wrote the following:

QUALIFICATIONS
A professional communicator with 10 years' experience in publishing and direct mail.

Embellished version:

A tenacious and collaborative problem solver with an investigative nature. Ten years in publishing and direct mail.

Share Juicy Facts That Support Your Objective
For example, one young woman I knew who had just graduated from college wanted to go into financial investing. She had paid for her entire college through financial investments she made. Well what does that say about her? A lot. So it went on her resume in the "Qualifications" section like this:
• *100% of education self-financed through financial investments.*

SUMMARY
• Don't be afraid to toot your own horn, even if it seems boastful.
• Spice up your writing with specific things you've accomplished, personal traits that make you stand out from everyone else, interesting tidbits that support your objective, active not

passive verbs and adjectives and adverbs.

- Be your own editor. Look for ways to be concise and clear. Eliminate unnecessary *a*'s, *an*'s and *the*'s. Use phrases instead of complete sentences. Say exactly what you mean. Trim excess words, and get rid of jargon.
- Big don'ts: Humor, business babble, sounding too good to be true, photographs, colleagues' and bosses names and phrases that say zilch.

- Look for ways to incorporate words and phrases that hit today's employers' hot buttons.
- Simplify descriptions of your experience. Don't assume readers know what a "multifunctional team to evaluate and recommend short/long-term trade spending strategies to integrate products including off-invoice allowances" means. Put it in English. Pretend your mother will read this.

chapter six

Clearing Up Simple Misunderstandings

Even though you're deciding what ends up on your resume, you're not going to rewrite history, cook up experience, lie, distort facts or disregard basic information people expect to see.

You are merely selecting information that's relevant and what you'll highlight or downplay to get across what you want the reader to know about you (see your thesis statement from chapter three, or hopefully it's on the wall in front of you).

This is the only smart thing to do because your resume, after all, is a marketing tool that helps position you the way you want.

But like it or not, you probably have some "perceived liabilities." These are facts about you and your career that could be misunderstood. In other words, someone who's looking for reasons to disqualify you from the running might use them, well, to do just that. So let's try to minimize the odds of that happening.

For you optimists in the world, this is the chapter where you'll learn how to build on your background, circumstances and dynamics of your career, instead of shunning certain parts.

For you pessimists, ask yourself if any of your "liabilities" would keep you from performing well if you actually got the job.

WHAT WORRIES YOU

Let's get it out on the table right here. Just what are you worried that an employer might not take kindly to? See if any of these sound familiar. You:

- Are over fifty
- Have gaps between jobs
- Left the workforce (for whatever reason)
- Got your degree later in life
- Never finished your degree
- Don't have any higher education
- Have advanced degrees that might scare off some employers
- Have been out of the field you want to get back into
- Have little or no experience in the field you want to get into (you just graduated, have been a homemaker, are making a career change)
- Have job titles that don't reflect your work
- Got all your experience at one company
- Have experience that goes back twenty years
- Were only at a job a few months
- Had a lot of jobs in a short time
- Left a company during a downsizing (by choice or you got the old heave-ho)
- Had mostly temp jobs or been a contract employee

I want to stress several things before we go on:

- You cannot hide the facts of who you are and what you've done.
- These facts do not mean there's anything wrong with you. I bring them up because you may think they are problems or worry that employers would.
- You may be worrying about these unnecessarily. No one but you may care.
- None of these circumstances may apply to you. Please read this chapter anyway. You can still get ideas on how to position yourself better.
- No matter how well you highlight and de-emphasize certain points, you can't control how someone will react. You can only influence someone's perception.
- There are no absolute right ways to accomplish your goal, which is to minimize misunderstandings. The following tips have proved useful to my clients.

Fifty-Plus Issue

Some employers think so-called older workers won't be good employees for the following possible reasons:

- They won't be up-to-date on new technology in their fields.
- They don't understand computers.
- They're not flexible and open to change.
- They'll want too much money.

If you're worried any or all of these will be obstacles, don't advertise your age. Some suggestions:

- Don't list the year you graduated from college.
- Don't list the years you worked in various positions. (This could also raise suspicions. If you're on the fence with this, don't do it.)
- Limit your experience to the last fifteen years. (Some jobs may be so long ago, they don't have much relevance anyway.) You can—but don't have to—call this "Recent Experience."
- Lump together earlier experience with a statement like, "Earlier experience includes ten years in public relations."
- Stay away from words like *senior executive*.

IN OR OUT?

When you're trying to figure out what to keep or discard, weigh the significance of the event or experience. For example, perhaps early in your career you were promoted throughout the first three levels of your company in five years, when the average progression would be ten years. Maybe you received awards for your earlier work, got special assignments or were sponsored for postgraduate research. Even though they happened a while back, they're probably worth mentioning.

Another thing to consider: Let's say you want to show that you've got first-hand experience in all company functions. But that was twenty years ago when you got that experience. (You worked for a large company that rotated you through finance, marketing, operations, engineering and product development.) The last twelve years, you've specialized in operations. You still want to make reference to your earlier experience because it shows you've had firsthand experience in all areas of the company.

On the other hand, emphasize the types of things employers would be looking for: how you've stayed current in your field, computer courses you've taken and software you know and personal characteristics that emphasize flexibility and loyalty.

DONE BEING THE BIG CHEESE

What if, even though you've been one, you're not going after a top management position? I've had over-fifty-year-old clients who could care less about being in management positions like they previously held. They really just wanted a staff job.

One man was trying to get a job as a bank teller. He had been using a resume that touted his years of high-level management experience, descriptions of his sales presentations to senior management and enormous budgets he handled. He got nowhere. He scared off everyone. In his case, he needed to soft-pedal that experience.

We toned down his resume, eliminating wording like "Senior management professional with thirty years' experience." Instead, we called him "a mature and results-oriented problem solver." We focused on his knowledge of business operations and developing satisfied customers and talent for building goodwill.

My father, who is a retired dentist, wanted to work part time in a position where he could be around people and talk to them. (You can imagine why, after all those years of stuffing cotton in people's mouths and not being able to hold a decent conversation with anybody.) Today he's a part-time representative for a waterproofing company. He goes to malls and county fairs and places like the Zucchini Festival in Obetz, Ohio, where he talks to people about their kids, grandkids, their houses and their leaky basements.

In other words, it's his ability to develop rapport with complete strangers that makes him effective and got him this job. He also has a strong work ethic, is honest and dependable as all get out and knows what it takes to run a business since he owned one for forty years. So these are things he'd emphasize on his resume.

Remember, go back to your positioning statement: How do you want them to see you? Then use language and examples to support that.

WHEN AGE IS RELEVANT

A recruiter told me age is only relevant in terms of career potential and upward mobility. For example, if he was going to hire a draftsperson and wanted someone with no expectation to be an engineer or designer, he'd hire an older worker who he knew wouldn't get bored. It's pretty certain that a twenty-two-year-old with a degree would be bored after a year.

Or take a fifty-five-year-old with a thirty-year career and a resume that indicates no career advancement. To a prospective employer, that says something about the person's level of achievement. If the employer is looking for someone who wants to advance, he probably wouldn't choose him.

What can you do about the perception of "wanting too much money"? Not much on your resume. The best you can do is cross that bridge when you come to it in the interview.

Gaps Between Jobs or Left the Workforce

Way back in chapter one, I talked about how you may have taken time off from a "traditional" career path. If the experience was positive and enhanced your life, look for ways to incorporate it in your resume.

One of my clients worked and traveled in Europe for a year after college graduation. We listed several of her experiences—full-time jobs and freelance work—on her resume. In fact, because of this experience, we were able to describe her as having hands-on experience with culturally diverse groups of people and international cultures.

When you have unexplained gaps, it might get an employer wondering, "Hmmm, I wonder what Zoe was doing between 1994 and 1995." In other words, it's not obvious by looking at your resume what you were doing when you weren't working.

If the gaps are only months, you alleviate any misperception by listing years, not the months, at your various jobs anyway.

My experience has been that if your resume is strong, most employers won't screen you out because of unexplained gaps. But they may bring them up in interviews. So be prepared to address them.

There's usually a perfectly good explanation. You could have had an illness or surgery, dealt with an ill family member, had a child, taken time off to raise your family, gone back to school, taken a sabbatical or decided to conduct an in-depth look at your next career move.

Don't worry about it. Some people still want to add explanations on the resume, such as "Returned to school for two years" or whatever. I don't think the resume is the place for it.

For one thing, you start sounding defensive. Two, you may bring up something the reader had never even thought about and create a problem. Three, when you bring attention to it, you make a mountain out of a molehill.

And like I said before, if you did go back to school, your education section will reflect that.

Got Your Degree Later in Life

I can't think of any downside. It shows you're determined and goal oriented. If you're concerned it will draw attention to your age, don't list your graduation date.

Never Finished Your Degree

Are you worried someone will think you don't follow through or complete things you start? Well, I suppose an employer could think that. Or are you worried that employers only want people with degrees? Some do make it a prerequisite.

First of all, if you don't have your degree, you don't have it. And for the moment, nothing is going to change that. And if you don't plan to get it, then that's that. So I'd spend time on your own brain just accepting this fact of your life. That makes it less of an issue and easier for you to concentrate on enhancing what you *do* have.

Other things you can do:

• Indicate the education you have by saying:
Two years studying business, including courses in accounting, management development, DOS and Lotus.
Miami University   1987-1989

Marketing classes, University of Cincinnati
1994-1995

• Add continuing education classes on the job. If you're still planning to complete your degree say something like:
Business courses toward attainment of Associates in Business Administration
University of Rhode Island

Real-life experience is invaluable, so emphasize results of your experience.

For example, let's say you've been in sales and marketing and are interviewing for a new position. The types of companies you're targeting hire the cream of the crop, which, in your mind, means they'll want someone with a degree plus a stellar performance record. (You don't know for sure that the degree is an absolute requirement, you're just reading into it.)

Here's where you emphasize your performance and results of your work anywhere you can on your resume.

In your qualifications:

Results-oriented professional with proven track record in implementing aggressive sales and marketing programs that dramatically increased sales, profits and market share. Expertise includes:

• Strategic marketing
• Product positioning

• Distribution
• Technical sales
• Sales presentations
• National account contracts
• Forecasting and budgeting
• Proposal development

Then prove those words with specific examples *in your accomplishments*:

• Developed new four-state territory that generated $22 million in new business in eight months.
• Realigned product line and pricing structure that significantly enhanced efficiency of internal operations and increased sales by 40%.

Don't Have Any Higher Education

It's the same kind of situation as the last one. If you don't have any intention of going to school, then so be it.

• Emphasize your on-the-job experience and results of your efforts.
• List any on-the-job training.
• In most cases, don't list your high school.

Have Advanced Degrees That Might Scare Off Employers

If you're worried someone will feel threatened by your education or that you're overqualified, you can do one of several things.

• Definitely don't put your advanced degree after your name at the top of the resume. I had a client who was very proud of his Ph.D. and insisted it go in large bold letters after his name. You couldn't miss it. When I brought up how an employer might react to this announcement, he didn't care. His ego got in the way.
• You could omit your degree from your resume (under the "Education" section). It's just an idea. But if you know it's an issue with a particular company, it's something to consider.

A human resource professional from a large company was quick to point out this: Not mentioning your advanced degree may get you an initial interview, but the fact that you have the degree will eventually become known during the hiring process or later on the job. This could get a little touchy. You see, some companies actually have salary structures that *require* a particular salary level for certain degrees. So you don't want to leave it off job applications. But it is something you can leave off your resume.

Been Out of the Field You Want to Get Back Into

An employer might worry you're out of the loop, don't have the necessary skills and aren't up on the latest trends and techniques in the field.

There are several ways to bring more attention to what you have, as opposed to what the employer thinks you might lack.

To illustrate this, let's pretend you started out working on the administrative side of education. You've been in teaching the last couple years and want to get back into administration.

Think through and incorporate the following:

• What skills does this field require? It might include managing and problem solving related to personnel and operations; organizing and following through on plans and other details; effective communications; being a team player. Have you been doing any of that while you've been teaching? Of course you have.

The skills it takes to do this job aren't necessarily that different than what you've been doing. They've just been in a different setting—the classroom.

• What have you done that will illustrate these skills? For instance, think of one or two examples of how you've organized and followed through on plans and details. Did you organize any class projects, parent-teacher programs or special events? What was the result?

• What knowledge do you need for this type of position? For starters, I'd list supervision, management, educational laws and statutes that affect administrative services, parent-teacher relations. My guess is, if you've been in education, you know these subjects. If not, you need to bone up on them.

• What type of person does well in this kind of job? In other words, what personal characteristics and qualities does it take to be effective? Patience, attention to detail, thoroughness, dedication, decisiveness are a few that come to mind. (Look back at

chapter two where you wrote "How others describe you.")

You'll notice the four points I just listed are the things people look for from chapter one: What can you do? Have you done it and stuck with it? What do you know? What kind of person are you?

• Include examples of volunteer or community work where you've demonstrated these skills.
• List courses you've taken, such as computer classes, and professional organizations you belong to that show how you've kept up-to-date.
• Emphasize these skills and examples by organizing your experience by function rather than mere chronological order. (See functional resume format in chapter four.)

Have No Experience or Haven't Worked Outside the Home for a Long Time

NEW GRADUATE:

• It's usually a good idea to put your degree at the beginning of your resume in the "Qualifications" section, especially if your education supports the type of career you're going after.
• Emphasize recognition and honors you've received, school and community activities and leadership positions you've held.
• List jobs you had during college. If you are going from high school into the job market, list jobs you had during school.

HOMEMAKERS AND GRADUATES:

• Emphasize internships, volunteer work and any gratis work that's relevant. To help the reader see how your work made a difference, give the results of your contribution.

For example, don't just say you volunteered for the March of Dimes for ten years. Analyze your experiences as a volunteer or board member. What projects did you work on? Why was that important? What skills did that take? What difference did it make? Create accomplishments from this.

Once you've analyzed your experience, you can put something like this on your resume:

Developed pilot fund-raising program that
catapulted local nonprofit organization from

last in the country in fund-raising to number three in the country within first year of implementation.

As a homemaker, if you've managed your home and the activities of your family and planned and prepared meals, what skills did that take?

My mother manages a small retail store. She hadn't worked in retail for forty years. But when she went job hunting, she emphasized her ability to manage a home and family, successfully head countless community and volunteer projects and manage the business operations of my father's dental practice.

• Organize your experience by function or skills instead of chronological listing.

So, let's say for example you want to illustrate your skill as a project manager. The project at the March of Dimes that I just wrote about is a great way to do that.

CAREER CHANGERS:

• In general, emphasize internships, co-op and volunteer work and any gratis work that's relevant. Show the results of your contributions.

• Build on the experience that you have by showing the reader how it will make you effective in the new position you seek.

For example, let's say you're an accountant and want to be in operations. To show the reader you're a whole lot more than a bean counter, don't dwell on the nitty-gritty, daily activities of bean counting. Sure, you're going to acknowledge that as part of "What you know." But your objective is to position yourself as someone who can see a bigger picture and effectively handle all operations of a company.

So list accomplishments that show the bottom-line value to the operations of the entire company. Think through what skills it takes to oversee operations and what personal attributes would be important. If they fit, put them on your resume.

• If your early experience is in a field totally unrelated to the one you want to get into, or for whatever reason you don't want to go into great detail about it (it may have little or no relevance), put it under a

heading like, "Additional experience includes eight years in teaching."

Whether you're a new graduate, have been a homemaker or are changing careers, you need to see yourself as someone with skills and talents that can transfer into a new environment. Your experiences—whether you were paid or not—are valuable. That's one reason I suggest you identify the section of your resume that lists your experience (paid or not) as "Experience," rather than "Employment History." Remember, you're trying to show your potential.

Weird Job Titles

If your job titles don't reflect the work you've done, here are some suggestions:

• Organize your experience by function.
• Change your titles so they better illustrate what you did.

For example, if your title was Secretary and your duties were assisting your boss on a variety of administrative tasks, change it to Administrative Assistant. Or you could use both: Administrative Assistant/Secretary. (See chapter two under "What Do They Call You, and What Do You Do All Day?" for more details.)

Experience Is at One Company

Odds are, you had different positions at this company. So:

• Emphasize the various jobs and areas of knowledge you gained.
• Depending on your career objective, this may be another one of those times when you break down your experience by function.

One of my clients had been with a Fortune 500 firm for fourteen years. Her technical expertise and education were in information technology. But she had loads of experience in training and management and enjoyed that the most. At this point in her career, she wanted to be a consultant. Her skills and knowledge in all three areas made her well qualified.

Her old resume made her sound like a techno-nerd. We needed to show she was a key decision maker who understood the business functions of a complex organization and had extensive experience in training and leadership. So when we wrote her qualifications, we organized her expertise into three areas: training, management and information technology. Then we gave examples of each of those areas in her experience.

- Give examples of your other interests and involvement in the community.

Experiences Goes Back Twenty Years

- Use your thesis statement to decide what to include.
- Think about how relevant some of your earlier experience is.

For example, if you've been in information technology for the past fifteen years and twenty years ago you started out as a retail buyer, you probably wouldn't put that early experience on your resume.

- See the fifty-plus issue dilemma.

Only in a Job a Short Time

If you were at a job a few weeks or months, you don't have to list it.

If, however, you're asked to complete a formal job application, give a complete and accurate representation of your background, education and experience. You're going to be signing it, attesting to its accuracy.

Had a Lot of Jobs

First decide which jobs you're going to list because they support your objective.

- See if there's a way to group together jobs into particular categories, such as customer service, marketing, sales.

When that hasn't been possible, I've used the heading "Other Experience" and listed some of the positions there. You don't have to describe the details of every job either. For that matter, you don't have to give any details if you don't want.

If you've had several positions that are similar at different firms, you can do this: Inventory Clerk Frammingham Plastics . . . Lightweight Lamps, Inc. . . . Socko Computers

Left During a Downsizing

Depending on who you worked for, you could have been "released," "involuntary separated," "rightsized," "reshaped," "reduced" or "payroll adjusted." Or you could have just left because you simply couldn't stand it anymore. This is another one of those situations you leave to a face-to-face discussion. The employer doesn't know by looking at your resume that you left by choice or got the sackaroo.

Had Mostly Temp Jobs or Been a Contract Employee

If you've only worked for many different companies through a temporary agency or as a contract employee, you can categorize your jobs by the type of work you did or title, describe the assignments and list your achievements. For example:

Test Engineer, Lemming's Personnel 1994-Present Lebanon, Wisconsin
Evaluate product performance and design durability for Roget's Products, Division of General Engineering, Cyber Products, Division of Bowes and Bowes.

- Analyzed performance and construction of six competitive windowlift motors that will significantly reduce motor design cost.

If you have a combination of temporary or contractual and full-time positions, you can list the temporary assignments like I just described or by the companies you worked for directly. If you do the latter, indicate that it was a temporary assignment.

Otherwise, you could really tick off an employer if she thinks you were trying to snow her.

EXPERIMENT 'TIL YOU GET IT RIGHT

You may start out writing your resume one way, then change it because you got a reaction you didn't want.

For example, Molly was one of my clients who had worked in the Catholic diocese most of her career. She had three different positions in this system. Now she wanted a job in a public setting. Most people zeroed in on her experience in this system and just couldn't imagine her anywhere else.

The first thing we did was dramatically change the language she used to describe her experiences. Then we looked for ways to emphasize her experience in education, instead of where she did it. This first version looked like this:

Assistant Director, Adult Education   1993-1996
<u>Diocese of Cleveland</u>, Cleveland, Ohio
Oversaw admissions program for nonprofit organization that provided adult education. Recruited students, planned curriculum, coordinated state conferences. Trained staff, students and faculty. Evaluated student progress.

Education Coordinator   1987-1992
Assisted in development of adult education program. Oversaw promotion and public relations. Recruited students and faculty.

Educational Program Coordinator   1982-1986
Coordinated educational program for elementary and high school students.

Personnel Representative   1980-1982
<u>Libby & Lu's Personnel Services</u>, Akron, Ohio
Interviewed applicants, conducted skills assessment tests and selected temporary employees for clients.

The idea was to emphasize the position and downplay the diocese. So we put her title in bold and her employer under that. To be consistent, though, we had to present all her jobs the same way. Well, the strategy worked, sort of. We were successful in bringing more attention to her jobs, but people thought these jobs were at different companies and that she jumped around a lot. She was concerned about this, so we rewrote it to look like this:

<u>Diocese of Cleveland</u>, Cleveland, Ohio   1982-1996

Assistant Director, Adult Education   1993-1996
Oversaw admissions program for nonprofit organization that provided adult education. Recruited students, planned curriculum, coordinated state conferences. Trained staff, students and faculty. Evaluated student progress.

Education Coordinator   1987-1992
Assisted in development of adult education program. Oversaw promotion and public relations. Recruited students and faculty.

Educational Program Coordinator   1982-1986
Coordinated education program for elementary and high school students.

<u>Libby & Lu's Personnel Services</u>, Akron, Ohio

Personnel Representative   1980-1982
Interviewed applicants, conducted skills assessment tests and selected temporary employees for clients.

By the way, there was never a misunderstanding with this version.

One More Word on Where You Put What

I've talked a lot about how and where to put information so it best presents you. But don't forget the tendency of most people when they read resumes. A human resource director put it like this:

I usually scan a resume and look mostly at the top half of it. So put the most important things first: your objective, work experience and how you've made a difference. Education is secondary, yet everyone puts it first.

NOT TO WORRY

I've known people with no degree and little or no experience in a particular field who landed a great job. I've met people switching careers who found their ideal position in just four months. They usually have several things in common.

1. They don't worry about their "liabilities." They are aware of them but focus more on what they want and what they do have.
2. As a result, they create marketing tools—resumes and what they verbally say about themselves—that focus on what they do have, not what they lack.
3. They put most of their energy into getting out and talking to people—they hold informational meetings. Therefore, people meet the real-live person first, not the resume. They leave the resume with the people after the meetings.

My point is, if you're conducting a thorough and effective job search, you don't rely totally on your resume to speak for you. It supports you. These "liabilities" are less of a sticky point if an employer can see and sense the whole person.

SUMMARY

If an employer is looking for reasons to disqualify you from the running, she might use your "perceived liabilities" to make a case. These are facts about you and your career that could be misunderstood. They include gaps between jobs, no college education to no experience or having a lot of jobs in a very short time.

You can't hide the facts of who you are and what you've done. And you can't control how someone will react. But you can influence perception. So try to minimize misunderstandings by highlighting some things and de-emphasizing others.

Always look for ways to build on what you do have. Keep referring back to your thesis statement to decide what to include or exclude.

CONCERN	POSSIBLE SOLUTIONS
Are an "older worker"	• Don't list college graduation date • Don't list dates of past positions • Limit experience to last fifteen years • Group together earlier experience under heading without listing each job • Don't say "senior executive" • Emphasize how you've stayed current: computer courses and other education • Emphasize flexibility and work ethic
Gaps between jobs	• List years, not months at your jobs • Create such a darn strong resume it's not an issue
Got degree later in life	• Don't list graduation date
Never finished degree	• Accept the fact that you don't have it • List education you did get • List continuing education on the job • Indicate if you plan to complete it • Emphasize results of your work experience
No higher education	• Accept the fact of your situation • Emphasize your on-the-job experience and results • List on-the-job training
Have advanced degrees	• Don't list in prominent place on resume • Don't list on resume at all
Been out of the field you want to get back into	• Think through what skills you need, ways you've demonstrated those skills, knowledge you need and personal characteristics it takes for the job • Give examples of volunteer and community work that demonstrate these skills • List courses you've taken and other ways you've stayed up-to-date • Organize experience by function
Have no experience	*New grads*: • Put degree under qualifications • List recognition and honors, school and community activities and leadership positions held, internships and relevant gratis work • Give results of your work • Organize experience by function or skills *Career changers*: • Emphasize internships, co-op and volunteer work, relevant gratis work • Show results of your work • Build on your past experience, even if not directly related

CONCERN	POSSIBLE SOLUTIONS
	Been a homemaker: • List volunteer work and relevant gratis work • Give results of your work • Organize experience by function or skills • Show how abilities to manage home and volunteer projects transfer into marketable skills
Weird job titles	• Organize experience by function • Change titles to illustrate your work
Experience at one company	• Emphasize various jobs and areas of knowledge • List experience by function • List other interests and community involvement
Experience goes back twenty years	• Decide what to include based on your thesis statement • Evaluate how relevant earlier experience is
Only in job a short time	• Don't list it
Had lots of jobs	• Group together jobs in categories like customer service, marketing, sales • Group some jobs under "Other Experience" • Group several companies together under job title
Left during downsizing	• Discuss this in interview, not on your resume
Had temp jobs or been contract employee	• Categorize jobs by type of work you did or title • List achievements

Looking Good

n the advertising business, I learned not only the importance of good writing, but good looking. See, you can write a wonderful ad, brochure or annual report, but if it doesn't look easy to read, people won't get to the first, let alone second, line. Same goes for your resume.

So here's where you'll learn to make important stuff stand out and tips on making a resume so readable, you'll get the employer to scan your resume and then find it appealing enough to put in the "keeper" pile. You'll achieve that if, when she first picks up your resume, it's easy to read. She may not even realize why. It just feels inviting. Here are some ways to do that.

A FEW OF MY FAVORITE THINGS
White Space

This is just what it sounds like: places on the page where there is nothing but the paper itself. It's like breathing room. It helps the reader's eye move down the page and on to important information. You can create white space by writing phrases instead of complete sentences. Also, double-space between the various sections of your resume.

Bullet Points

Bullets are a nice way to highlight single words and phrases. I also like to give a few spaces after a bullet point. Just makes it easier on the eye.

Indentations

They make bigger blocks of words more readable. Indents also indicate a new thought.

Columns and One-Inch Margins on Each Side

This breaks up a string of words and, again, makes it easier to read.

Here's an example of how all these techniques used together make a difference.

Inviting:

OBJECTIVE

A leadership position that contributes to the efficiency of daily operations and uses proven strengths to:

- Coordinate flow of operations
- Oversee personnel functions
- Follow through on details and tasks
- Lead staff to reach goals and objectives
- Communicate effectively with diverse groups of people

Uninviting:

OBJECTIVE

A leadership position that will contribute to the efficiency of daily operations and uses proven strengths to coordinate flow of operations, lead staff to reach goals and objectives, follow through on details and tasks, communicate effectively with diverse groups of people and oversee personnel functions.

Isn't the inviting example much easier to scan and get a sense of what you can offer?

MORE TIPS FOR READABILITY

• Underline job titles or company names to differentiate or highlight. But be consistent. If you underline titles in your present position, underline them in all the others too.

• Keep the same margins throughout your resume. The only time I change a margin is if a phrase goes to another line. Example:

All areas of banking, including investments, government regulations and financing.

• Use the same typeface on your entire resume. I like serif typefaces, rather than sans serif. Serif typefaces have little "feet" that make it easier for your eye to slide from one word to the next. Most daily newspapers and magazines use serif type.

Advertising guru David Ogilvy used a Gallop poll to survey and document that serif type was easier to read by a larger percentage of people than sans serif. So he insisted that all the copy in his ads use serif type. This book is set in a serif type. Look at the difference between these two examples:

Serif Typeface:

All areas of banking, including investments and financing

Sans Serif Typeface:

All areas of banking, including investments and financing

• Use a letter-quality printer to print your resume. Near letter-quality and dot matrix printers don't cut it. Once you've got a dark, crisp original of your resume, take it to a copying place that has a high-quality copier. Or just print out copies as you need them.

• Use white, cream or light gray paper in a 10-pound weight with a linen or laid finish or something similar. I've seen resumes on paper that looks like it has little flecks of lint on it. This looks too casual. You're trying to be as classy as possible. You know how you're going to wear your nicest, most conservative suit to the interview? Well, your resume is like that. Present it on the finest, most professional paper you can. And make sure your envelope and letterhead match.

MORE TIPS

• Double-check phone numbers and addresses. This is where I usually find errors. (This can make you look real stupid.) The trouble is, most people just don't proofread numbers like they should.

• Use spell check if you're typing on a computer. But don't forget, it doesn't know if you've used the correct word. For example, you meant to use the word *meet*, but the word on the page is *meat*. Spell check won't pick that up.

• It also doesn't know the difference between *your* and *you're*. One more thing: Whenever you make a change, whether it's retyping a single word or an entire line, always use your spell checker again. It's incredibly easy to make errors.

• Proofread your resume starting at the end of a sentence. You're less apt to miss errors because you're concentrating on each word instead of the meaning of a phrase or sentence.

• Don't just proofread on your computer screen. Things look different when you see them on the printed page. So print out your resume—then proof it. You'll notice extra spaces between words, bullets that aren't lined up and lines that look too short. When you're typing on a computer and, especially, when you're creating columns, it's always amazing to me how a single keystroke can goof everything else up. So look for these kinds of errors every time you change something.

• Read it out loud. You'll notice typos more readily because reading aloud keeps you from scanning.

• Hold your resume a couple feet in front of you and view it as a whole. Do the pages look balanced? Is your eye drawn to the parts you want to stand out? Is it easy to move from one section to the next? Overall, does it look easy to read?

• There's no excuse for smudges, typographical errors, tears and dog-eared corners. When you ship off your resume, it should look immaculate. Keep copies in a folder where they stay flat.

• Show your resume to at least one more person to scan for anything you might have overlooked.

Now you're ready to photocopy it.

BEFORE YOU MAKE ONE HUNDRED COPIES

It's hard to say how many versions it will take before you get your resume the way you want it. But count on many rewrites.

I've been a writer most of my career, and it takes me five, six, sometimes eight tries to get the words just right. (I rewrote that sentence four times.) After I write an article, resume, letter or whatever, I leave it alone for a day or two. Then I come back to it and can't believe I missed some major typographical error. I'm totally embarrassed by a sentence that seemed perfectly fine the day before and thank the stars I didn't mail it like that. I mess with it some more. Leave it alone. Then I come back to it and find yet another typo. Show it to someone whose opinion I trust. Then go back to it again.

RESUMES THAT GO TO AND FRO ELECTRONICALLY

If I didn't talk about this aspect of resumes, you might think I am a technophobe. You are absolutely correct. (Even though I've worked on a computer since 1984, I still worry mine will blow up any moment.)

This electronic stuff, though, is one more tool available to you. And if you use these techniques, I want you to do it right. So I tried to put into as simple English as possible the options you have and how to use them. Some of these ideas may not be a good choice for you. I'll talk about why in a minute.

First, let's define what it means to send or receive resumes electronically.

Thanks to technology, companies can hunt for employees via computer. How many people actually get jobs this way is still questionable. But companies—especially larger ones—are tapping into this automated resource three ways:

1. By listing available positions on their Web pages, the commercial portion of the Internet.

2. By listing positions via online career center job listings. These are databases on the Internet to which companies pay a nominal fee to advertise available jobs.

3. By posting positions through Usenet groups, also known as bulletin boards. For example, if you were looking for a job in Chicago, you'd go to *chi.jobs* on the Internet to find jobs that are available there. These are fading in popularity because there are just too many listings and they're difficult to navigate.

You, of course, respond to these postings. (I'll talk about how in a second.) But you can also post your resume in a database for a fee that ranges from $5 to $15. And if someone likes what he sees, he gets in touch with you.

You may have heard that only high-tech jobs—anything related to computer systems—get posted on the Internet. Well, according to Bill Warren, president of Online Career Center—the largest career center on the Internet—two years ago that was pretty much the case. Something like 94 percent of the jobs listed were technical in 1995.

But by mid-1996, only about 61 percent of the jobs were technical. The rest of the openings apply to the rest of the work world. For example, Procter & Gamble posted jobs that ranged from a human safety scientist position in Caracas, Venezuela, to a part-time dining room employee in Cincinnati.

The reason: The World Wide Web has become more accessible to individuals in their homes. Companies can now reach people besides techies, who mainly discovered these positions at their computers at work.

Employers like it because they can reach job hunters from coast to coast and pretty cheaply, at that.

You can respond to these openings by sending your resume:

• Directly to the company via e-mail, fax or U.S. mail, or, as some people call it, snail mail. (See chapter one.)

• As a text file as part of an e-mail message, or as an attachment (that's computer lingo for other information you send with your e-mail message).

According to people much more knowledgeable than I am about these things, most of the time it's best to send your resume as an ASCII text file—not as an attachment—since the receiver may not have the software to convert the file and read it.

• On the Internet by a process called file transfer protocol (ftp). For now, this is not used very often because the receiver needs special software.

Sometimes, a company wants you to complete an application online. Read the instructions the company gives so you know how they want to receive your resume.

Companies also use resume database services—these services collect resumes for employers who are their clients—in which you fax or e-mail your resume or complete their lengthy applications online.

So you are sending your resume electronically when you use e-mail or complete an application online.

Sometimes, it's a computer—not a person—that gets your resume. In that case, you've just sent your resume to a company with special resume scanning technology that reads your resume and zeros in on keywords and phrases that tell it you have the skills to do the job. So you need to send a resume that's compatible or considered an "electronic resume." I'll talk about how to do that in a minute.

Electronic industry experts feel this scanning technology will be used less as more people understand and use electronic options.

Even if you don't send you resume electronically, some companies will scan it into their internal computer management systems later. In that case, you may want to send an electronic resume, plus your printed one. So, you should ask a company how your resume will be handled.

How to Write an "Electronic" Resume

Again, that's a resume that can be read by special optical scanning equipment. The authors of *Electronic Resume Revolution*, Joyce Lain Kennedy and Thomas J. Morrow, describe this tracking computer as a "hard-nosed tool. It is interested only in provable facts, measurable quantities, and recognizable nouns, including industry jargon."

Therefore, your "electronic resume" has to look like what the computer is programmed to find. As the authors say, you have to play by the system's rules.

The rules require you to use what are called "keywords." These are buzzwords that help the computer figure out how to label you. These are nouns, not verbs. They can be skills, education or a particular college.

The more of these buzzwords you have, the more likely you'll be selected by the computer as a candidate for the job. Read the ad for the position you found on the Internet to pick up these buzzwords.

If the ad doesn't give a lot of detail, think about what skills, education, knowledge and experience the job would require.

For example, if you were applying for a bookkeeping job, keywords might include *accounts payable, accounts receivable, payroll, payroll tax, collections, general ledger, reconciliation of bank statements and accounts, financial reports, data entry, Associates Degree, Lotus 1-2-3, Windows.*

The rules also include making your resume scannable. This means no underlined type, graphics, italics, shading, abbreviations—except for buzzwords in your particular field—and in some cases, no bullets or boldface type. If the computer can't read your resume, it may send it back. Apparently computers, like people, also like white space.

If you are developing an electronic resume and need more detail, check out *Electronic Resume Revolution* or Jack Wright's book, *Resumes for People Who Hate to Write Resumes.* I've included a sample resume on page 74.

Is Electronic the Way to Go?

That depends. If you're in a technical field, absolutely. Most technical positions are posted online. And if you're not able to apply for a position online, it looks worse than bad to an employer. "It spells disaster as far as looking for a job," says Pam Dixon, author of *Be Your Own Headhunter Online.*

Techies are even expected to send thank-you notes via e-mail. It tells the employer you really know the workplace. Paper is out for techies.

The only exception to this rule is if you're working through a headhunter. Then you need to submit a paper resume.

For the rest of you, electronic job hunting can be one more aspect of your overall job search. More and more employers are definitely posting jobs online. There are now seminars for employers on how

Sample electronic resume

REGINA FOLDMASTER
111 Crestview Park
Hamden, Connecticut 06840
(204) 939-0000

SUMMARY OF SKILLS

Bookkeeping, accounts payable, accounts receivable, payroll, payroll tax, collections, general ledger, reconciliation of bank statements and accounts, financial reports, data entry, Associates Degree, Lotus 1-2-3, Windows.

OBJECTIVE

Position in bookkeeping that will utilize abilities to systematize financial data, work well under pressure, handle details and communicate with all levels of management and staff.

QUALIFICATIONS

Demonstrated abilities to develop simplified procedures and systems. Dedicated professional with a reputation for turning disorganized systems into profitable operations.

EXPERIENCE

The Winko Plastic Company   1989-Present
Hamden, Connecticut
Bookkeeper
Handle record keeping, accounts receivable, accounts payable, payroll and inventory control. Maintain ledgers and company checking account. Coordinate state audits.
- Reorganized bookkeeping system that saved thousands of dollars in late charges and turned idle money into high yielding investments.
- Developed financial system that helped firm pass two state audits with ease.

EDUCATION

Associates in Business Administration
University of Connecticut 1988

to recruit online. But like newspaper ads and working with recruiters, I don't recommend you spend all your time on it.

The pros:

• It's an easy and fast way to apply for a job. You don't have to write a letter, call anyone—initially anyway—or set up appointments. You don't have to mess with all that packaging of matching letterhead and mailing off a letter. And the employer can breeze through tons of resumes.

• You get exposure you may not otherwise have. You may discover positions that aren't advertised other ways. So go ahead and respond to openings you learn about online. Get your resume into a database or two. But don't rely on them soley.

• If you understand how to use this technology, you'll be better prepared for the next wave. And according to Bill Warren of Online Career Center, because of this new technology, you'll be able to manage your career online.

For example, his company recently implemented a system in which you not only put your resume online, but can edit, deactivate or activate it whenever you want. So if you go into work Monday and find out your department is being eliminated, and your resume has been deactivated, you simply reactivate it by clicking on the "activate" icon on your resume.

The new system also gives you more confidentiality because now you're identified solely by an e-mail address. You would know the name of the company that's interested in you before you release your name.

Finally, you can request to get e-mail whenever a new job in a particular field or geographic location opens up. So if you're interested in marketing jobs in the Midwest, you'll be notified when that Director of Marketing job at the Fairfax Plastic Company in Ohio opens up—that's *if* the company chooses to advertise it via an online database.

The cons:

• The odds of finding a job by putting your resume in an electronic resume bank are slim. The odds of finding a job by sending your resume in response to a company's posting on a website or career center job listing are also slim. You will be one of hundreds, perhaps thousands—just like you are when you answer an ad—responding to an opening.

• If a computer gets your resume (a company is using optical scanning equipment), the computer's goal is to find the right words and eliminate you if you don't have them. So if your skills can't be easily converted to marketable keywords, this type of resume and job hunting is not a good route to go.

• Confidentiality could be a problem. Most online computer centers will ask you which companies you don't want your resume sent to. But because a company logs onto the Internet from many different e-mail addresses, they can't ensure it won't ever land at a particular firm.

Also, when you put your resume in a public resume data bank, some people, such as recruiters, have been known to take those resumes and store them for long-term use. So it's quite possible, five years from now you'll get a phone call from someone who's tracking your career.

WHERE TO SPEND MORE TIME

I suggest you spend most of your time face-to-face with people you can leave your resume with. When you meet potential employers or people who may refer you to employers, the purpose and the result are very different. People get to actually see you, know you and, hopefully, like you. People like to help people they know and like. Employers like to hire people they know. As a result, this is still where most hiring takes place. (You also cut down on your competition.)

Many jobs are created when an employer meets someone she realizes can solve a problem she has or fulfill a future need.

Even Kennedy and Morrow state: "Computers, amazing as they are, still cannot come close to sorting people as effectively as human beings sort people. . . . Computers have no way to look for the unexpected. What computers expect is what they've been told to expect. Nothing more."

SUMMARY

Invite the employers to read your resume with:

• Lots of white space and bullet points
• One-inch margins all around the page

- Serif typeface
- The same typeface throughout the entire resume
- High-quality paper
- A letter-quality printer

Proofread and proofread, including phone numbers and addresses.

If you are responding to positions that have been posted on the Internet, find out exactly how the company wants to receive your resume.

Find out if your resume will be electronically scanned. If it is, you need to develop a resume that's compatible and has keywords and phrases.

chapter eight

The Real McCoy

can talk until I'm blue in the face but until you actually see what I've been yapping about all these chapters, it's hard to picture. So here's where you'll find completed resumes from people in different professions, many who felt they had an army of liabilities.

They are categorized four ways:

1. Alphabetically with an explanation of the person's situation and the job he wanted or reference to a perceived liability I discussed in chapter six (some people's circumstances are also liabilities—in their minds anyway).

This section is called "Resumes by Situation." You'll notice on some resumes that I've pointed out how certain phrases or parts help the person accomplish his goal. I also include an example of a networking resume. (See chapter one, where I talk briefly about informational interviews, for how this is used.)

2. Alphabetically by general category of profession. This section is called "Resumes by Profession."

3. New graduate resumes, in a section with that title.

4. Yechy resumes—just what they sound like and also what the section is called.

It's not possible to show a resume for every profession here. And that's not the purpose of this chapter. If you've done the exercises in the preceding chapters, you can now develop one that describes the job you want and takes into consideration what the reader is looking for.

Use these, like every example I've given so far, as a guide. Notice how information was organized and what was emphasized, depending on the person's goal or objective and specific circumstance.

One more thing. The names on these resumes are all made up from my imagination. Company names, many of the colleges, universities, street names and associations are also fictional.

Resumes by Situation

ADMINISTRATIVE SERVICES AND SUPPORT

Situation: Likes job, but person whose job she would move up to has no intention of leaving.
Job she wants: High-profile, responsible, diverse administrative position.

PENELOPE POST
5656 Livingstone Road
Kansas City, MO 64140
(816) 221-0000

OBJECTIVE

Says she's responsible

Administrative assistant position that utilizies strengths to:

Says she's responsible

- Work independently
- Create efficient systems and procedures
- Interact well with customers, staff and all levels and management
- Manage work flow
- Set priorities and meet goals in a timely fashion

QUALIFICATIONS

A dedicated and conscientious professional with a reputation as a thorough organizer and skillful problem solver. Known for turning chaotic work space into productive environment. Able to handle multiple projects. Work well under pressure. Capabilities include:

She's responsible

- Special event and meeting planning
- Domestic and international travel arrangements
- Microsoft 5.1, Harvard Graphics for Windows and shorthand
- Customer service
- Preparation of confidential documents and routine correspondence
- Inventory control
- Supervision
- Scheduling of executive's calendar

Can handle diverse tasks

EXPERIENCE

Longbach Society for Strategic Planning, Liberty, Missouri   1990-Present
Administrative Assistant
Handle international travel arrangements for four executives and visiting colleagues. Compile monthly reports, plan board meetings and quarterly seminars. Coordinate and oversee planning logistics of special events. Develop meeting agendas and support materials. Develop and maintain databases of new business. Serve as liaison between management and board members.
- Diplomatically handled dozens of potentially sensitive interactions with customers and company board members.

- Organized and planned three-day seminar for visitors from Europe and Asia that included room arrangements, coordination of speakers, travel and hotel accommodations and sight-seeing.
- Organized and coordinated national sales meeting with potential customer that landed account worth $900,000.

Second National Bank, Kansas City, Missouri   1985-1990
<u>Staff Assistant to Senior Vice President of Lending</u>
Oversaw Senior Vice President's travel schedule. Assisted with daily operation of department. Planned corporate meetings and conferences. Compiled operational status reports. Handled correspondence from Board members. Supervised two secretaries.
- Developed system for easily accessing accounts payable and payroll that cut retrieval time from one day to five minutes.
- Developed inventory system to track office equipment and supplies that increased efficiency by 35%.

EDUCATION

Certified Professional Secretary, Institute of Certifying Secretaries 1987
Continuing education includes Team Management and Communication Skills
Associates in Business, Kansas City Kansas Community College 1985

Potential liability: No degree. **ADVERTISING**

LANCE NEWTON _____
5267 West Central Park, Honolulu, Hawaii 96810 • Home: (808) 841-2222

OBJECTIVE
A position that utilizes a wealth of knowledge in marketing, communications, advertising and the political process in order to influence and motivate others, using proven abilities to:
• Create dynamic marketing and communication programs
• Conceive and implement persuasive political and marketing strategies
• Envision and bring ideas to reality from conception to completion
• Promote products, policies and services
• Write and communicate concepts, proposals and plans

QUALIFICATIONS
A highly creative, self-motivated leader and communicator with over 10 years in business-to-business, industrial and consumer promotion and knowledge of the political process known for his political astuteness and bold approaches to problem solving. Expertise includes:
• Advertising: Corporate identification, direct mail, trade shows
• Writing: Annual reports, brochures, broadcasting, proposal, speeches
• Market research and analysis   • Press conferences
• Media planning and relations   • Issue management
• Product development and sales   • Public relations
• Understanding of legislative process   • Public speaking

EXPERIENCE
Account Executive, Sorrento & Company.   1986-Present
Manage marketing communication activities for local, national and international clients ranging from health care to industrial computers for advertising agency doing $20 million in annual billings. Develop strategy and positioning for clients engaged in politically sensitive activities.

He produces what matters: results

ACHIEVEMENTS:
• Developed new client sales, resulting in $1 million in additional company billings.
• Created advertising campaign for industrial client, generating such enormous numbers of leads that company met annual sales goals in three months.
• Won nine awards for most effective industrial and business-to-business promotions in regional advertising competition.

Lance Newton, page 2

Co-chairman, Issue Development Committee, Luawa County Republican Party. 1985

More results

ACHIEVEMENTS:
• Conceived direct marketing campaign that increased voter turnout by way of absentee ballots by 100%.
• Devised strategy and targeted issues that were implemented into party's election platform, doubling the party's representation on City Council.

Co-chairman, Citizens for Responsible Government Spending.   1984

Results

ACHIEVEMENTS:
• Coordinated grassroots campaign and developed political strategy that resulted in highest percentage of vote ever recorded in city's history to defeat an earnings tax; saved taxpayers $12 million.
• Organized and held dozens of press conferences that generated lead stories in local newspaper editorial pages, *The Wall Street Journal* and coverage on television and radio.

EDUCATION
Marketing Communications, Hawaii State University 1981-1983
English/Creative Writing, University of Utah 1974-1977

MEMBERSHIPS
Board member, Business Professional Advertising Associates . . . Honolulu Marketing Association
Board member, March of Dimes, Honolulu, Hawaii

CONTROLLER/FINANCIAL ANALYST

> *Situation*: Had own accounting firm for the last twelve years.
> *Job he wants*: Controller, financial planning and analysis in corporation

LOGAN J. BRENNER
1515 Doodlebee Lane
Fairfax, Virginia 22033
(703) 803-2222

OBJECTIVE

To contribute to the profitable growth of an organization in the area of controlling, financial planning and analysis and financial systems and operations.

QUALIFICATIONS

Seventeen years in responsible fiscal operations and management as a consultant to service and start-up companies. Skilled liaison and take-charge leader. Known for ability to analyze complex financial data, build trusting relationships, lead others to achieve goals and clearly communicate. Speak fluent Spanish. Knowledge includes:

- Corporate tax planning and preparation
- Business valuation
- Auditing and internal control procedures
- Business plans and projections
- Management systems consulting
- Payroll
- Project management
- Finance
- Tax research
- Computer experience includes Microsoft Windows 2.1, Word, Excel, Timeslips and other application software for accounting and consulting practices

ACCOMPLISHMENTS

- Analyzed business operations of new wholesale business, selecting integrated management and accounting system and assisting in implementation that resulted in revenues of $30 million within 11 years.

- Converted manual accounting system of start-up computer firm to integrated system that included job costing; company tripled business volume within one year and today has over $10 million in revenues.

- Acted as liaison between owner of closely held company and new owner in business succession that involved business valuation and development of compensation package for former owner; result was smooth transfer of ownership and doubling of revenues the year transfer took place.

- Assessed tax ramifications for subsidiary of $8 billion company to invest in operations overseas; saved company from making costly decision.

EXPERIENCE

Brenner Certified Public Accountants, Fairfax, Virginia   1986-Present
<u>Owner</u>
Manage firm of four accountants and consult with businesses on tax planning and preparation and business planning including audits and projections, compilation and review of financial statements, business valuation and development of internal control procedures.

Lofting, Haughty & Nice, Certified Public Accountants, Washington, DC   1980-1985
<u>Staff Accountant</u>
Compiled financial statements for corporations, partnerships and trusts. Oversaw small business audits and prepared individual income tax returns.

EDUCATION

CPA Certificate 1979

Master of Business Administration 1984
Washington School of Management, George Washington University

B.S. in Accounting 1980
George Washington University

PROFESSIONAL MEMBERSHIPS

• American Society of Certified Public Accountants
• Washington Institute of Certified Public Accountants

Potential liability: No degree.   **CUSTOMER SERVICE**

BARRY BEALY
1462 Cottingham Court
San Ynez, CA 93461
(805) 687-2222

OBJECTIVE

Customer Service
To assist customers with problems concerning products or services, create harmonious and positive relations and contribute ability to build rapport, research and troubleshoot.

SUMMARY OF QUALIFICATIONS

- Diplomatic problem solver
- Reputation for following through until problem resolved
- Thorough understanding of order entry and processing
- Versed in product claims, customer credit, pricing
- Knowledgeable about shipping and receiving, inventory control

EXPERIENCE

Lamarnet, San Ynez, CA   1995-1997
Customer Service Representative
Handle 85 business accounts in three-state area. Troubleshoot service and billing problems. Consult with customers on product needs.

He's results-oriented
- Researched alternative pricing for long-time customer, saving $50,000 account.
- Turned around negative customer situation after misunderstanding concerning late payment, saving $25,000 account.
- Resolved customer's phone equipment problem that saved $45,000 account.

Mills Construction & Parts, Inc., San Ynez, CA   1988-1994
Account Representative
Quoted prices and reviewed claims with manufacturing and construction customers. Analyzed customer orders to determine production schedules and meet shipping requirements.
- Received Account Representative of the Year Award in 1990 and 1992.
- Solidified relationship with skeptical customer and increased new business by 20%.
- Researched dozens of shipping problems that ensured orders were received on time and construction project stayed on schedule.

Wolfgang Steel Brothers, San Ynez, CA   1982-1987
Customer Technical Representative
Handled service calls for customers in automotive, appliance and construction industry. Recommended products and oversaw claims resolution.

Assistant Account Representative   1981-1982
Handled data entry and updated customer mailing list.

EDUCATION

Classes in business and computer science, Greak Oaks Vocational Center 1991-1994

EDUCATION (ADMINISTRATION)

> *Situation*: Has had some experience in adminis-
> tration. Has had more experience as a teacher.
> *Job she wants*: A more responsible position as
> an administrator in a school system.

AMANDA ZEE
9092 Crater Lake
San Antonio, Texas 78201
(210) 736-2222

OBJECTIVE

A leadership position in education that will contribute to the efficiency of operations
while reducing costs and maintaining quality.

— Emphasizes administrative experience upfront

Qualified by 12 years in the classroom and day-to-day operations experience and broad
exposure to all facets of education. Committed to establishing fiscally sound policies.
Strengths to lead staff to reach goals and objectives, implement administrative details and
tasks and work cooperatively with superintendent, board members, staff and community.

Knowledge encompasses:
- Food services and building and grounds maintenance
- Purchasing
- Parent/teacher relations
- Short- and long-range planning
- Personnel hiring, evaluation, training
- Supervision
- Team building
- Knowledge of educational trends and innovations
- Financial planning and budgeting
- Texas regulations and statutes affecting education

*Gets more specific on
administrative knowledge*

EXPERIENCE

Assistant Principal   1995-Present
Vunderbar Elementary School, Franklin Schools, San Antonio, Texas
Assist in operation of 350-student elementary school with 20 teachers, 18 support staff,
including facilities maintenance, purchasing and personnel functions. Coordinate educational, professional development and community support programs. Design and present
in-service workshops. Conduct new employee orientations.

Amanda Zee, page 2

How her expertise paid off

- Led research, design and planning of new playground for outdoor equipment construction project that came in under budget and on time.
- Conducted cost analysis of classroom furnishings; purchased higher quality furniture than state bid list at a lower cost.
- Initiated weekly newsletter for parents, students and staff that significantly enhanced communication and established supportive relationships between school and community.
- Originated innovative program that increased parent and student participation and received statewide recognition for creative approach to parent involvement.
- Initiated state's first drug testing program at school district that requires athletes to prove they're drug free; expulsions due to drug-related activities have dropped 50%.

Department Chairperson, English Department
Teacher   1990-1994
Medford Middle School, Barney School System, San Antonio, Texas

- Developed and presented staff training on multimedia presentations that enhanced classroom learning and motivated students.
- Initiated and implemented new curriculum that incorporated multicultural and international writers and poets.
- Created in-service training for communication and team building skills.

Teacher   1985-1993
Loosewater Schools, Golearn School System, Dallas, Texas
Taught English at four elementary and middle schools.

Underscores hands-on experience in education

EDUCATION

Master of Education, Corpus Christi University 1992
Bachelor of Arts, Texas State University 1985

PROFESSIONAL ASSOCIATIONS

Member of Texas Association of School Administrators
Texas Teachers Association
American Association for Educational Administrators
American Society of Curriculum Development

ENGINEERING

> *Situation*: Last ten years have been temporary positions.
> *Job he wants*: Full-time position in electronic engineering and technical service.

JOHN ANGEL
8845 Padre Street
New Orleans, LA 70133
(504) 593-3333

Important to state since he wants full-time as a direct company employee.

OBJECTIVE

Full-time position in electrical engineering and technical services

PROFILE

Analytical problem solver with twelve years in electrical engineering and technical field service. Proven abilities to design electrical systems, troubleshoot electrical and computer problems and organize test data, distribution and power systems. Specific knowledge includes:
- Robotics
- CADD
- High voltage, security and antilock braking systems
- Solid state and mechanical distribution controls
- Industrial battery chargers
- Regulatory agency requirements

EXPERIENCE

Tiger Temporary, New Orleans, LA   1990-Present
Assignments include:

Electrical Engineer, **Mitchell and Bert Engineering, Inc.**   1995-1997
Research costs and implement design of power supplies, distribution, lighting and security systems.

Test Engineer, **General Development**   1993-1995
Evaluate product performance and durability per design specifications for antilock braking and windowlift systems.
- Analyzed performance and construction of twelve competitive windowlift motors that significantly reduce motor design cost.

Product Engineer, **Sylva Sisters, Inc.**   1990-1992
Modify electrical systems to be used in housing. Troubleshoot production line problems and evaluate customer requests for feasibility for industrial automatic guided vehicle battery chargers.
- Located trouble source of flickering light problem, eliminating problem that otherwise would have developed into critical situation.
- Designed electrical power center, initial distribution, fire alarm system, emergency electrical system and lighting for $6.5 million, seven-story renovation project.

New Orleans Gas & Electric, <u>Test Technician</u>, New Orleans, LA   1980-1989
Maintain solid state and mechanical distribution controls.

- Analyzed single line diagrams to test electrical system components without interrupting electrical service of 20,000 customers.
- Designed spreadsheet for quick retrieval of customer energy savings information that cut engineering time from two hours to ten minutes.

EDUCATION

B.S. in Electrical Engineering, Louisiana Technical Institute 1979

Professional Engineering Registration—Louisiana

MEMBERSHIPS

American Institute of Electrical Engineers

ENGINEERING/SYSTEMS ANALYST

Situation: Early experience and education in marketing; got second degree in Computer Engineering for new career.
Job she wants: Electrical and mechanical engineering.

DEMIE LESS
55 Falldown Lane
Alexandria, Virginia 22314
(703) 519-2222
E-mail: demieless@fuser.com

*Only use
e-mail address
if you check
it daily*

PROFILE

An analytical thinker and team player with a broad understanding of computers, electrical and mechanical engineering. Known for strengths to design detailed hardware and software systems, debug, document and implement computer applications for industry.

<u>Experience</u> includes real-time control systems and programming, digital logic design, integration of microprocessors and computers in analog systems.

<u>Knowledge</u> encompasses FORTRAN, Pascal, C, PL/1, Basic, Dbase III and PDP-11, 8080, 6800, 68000 Assembly Languages.

<u>Qualifications</u>: B.S. Computer Engineering, minor in Electrical Engineering
Virginia Polytechnic Institute and State University 1995
B.S. in Business Administration, Rockford State University 1987
Major: Operations Research and Quantitative Analysis

*Recent degree supports
new career objective*

ACHIEVEMENTS

• Designed electric motor testing using PDP-11/23 minicomputer, researched and selected new designs for motor shaft coupler and motor fixture that reduced test time by 85% and increased accuracy by 30%.

• Designed and programmed real-time operating system for PDP-11/05 computer system that significantly maximized throughput.

<u>College projects include</u>:
• Design and installation of digital control system on six degree-of-freedom robot that is used to teach Robotics class at London State University.
• Construction and testing of logic analyzer board for Z80 based microcomputer.

Demie Less, page 2

RELATED EXPERIENCE

<u>Engineer, Labador Systems, Inc.</u>, Alexandria, Virginia   1995-Present
Manage software solution process of DATSA/B1 program and provide computer support to track process for $15 billion mechanical design, automation, software and engineering services firm. Provide engineering support for automatic test equipment programs.

<u>System Analyst/Systems Engineer, Energy Institute</u>, Alexandria, Virginia   1994
Designed, installed and operated IBM computer system to establish new accounting system. Designed, installed and documented industrial test and measurement systems. Analyzed, designed and developed AS/400 software to support in-house software. Applied knowledge of RPGIII and CL.

<u>Earlier Experience includes</u>:

<u>Marketing Project Director, Bloomquist Research Co., Inc.,</u> Rockford, Illinois 1987-1993
Designed telephone and mail panel market research projects, estimated project costs. Wrote tabulation specification programs for projects and tested new software.

Potential liability: Older worker. **FINANCE**

GEORGIA O'KEATON
8922 Serenity Lane
Medford, Oregon 97503
(501) 773-2222

OBJECTIVE: Financial Management

To lead an accounting staff to create financial plans and systems that result in the sound and orderly financial operation of a business utilizing proven skills to:
- Plan budgets
- Control financial operations
- Analyze accounting data
- Write operating reports
- Communicate effectively with staff and management
- Systematize operating processes

QUALIFICATIONS

Wealth of knowledge in financial and business administration. Expertise includes:

- Accounting systems
- Budgeting
- Profit planning
- New facility planning

- Supervision
- Risk management administration
- Profit sharing and stock-option programs

ACCOMPLISHMENTS

- Designed and implemented functional cost accounting and budgeting system that gave senior management clear operating road map, product cost information and method for measuring performance.

- Planned and implemented bank branch expansion that allowed orderly growth from five to forty offices.

- Supervised financial control department with less than 2% turnover during 10-year period of massive changes in banking and automation during which time bank tripled assets.

- Interpreted complex SEC regulations that lead to permission to form and operate bank holding company.

- Managed bank's risk management program and increased deductible techniques resulting in increased commercial insurance coverage while premiums were reduced by 10%.

- Developed monitoring technique to track changes in selling price and cost of funds, providing spread analysis, a vital operating statistic for senior management.

Georgia O'Keaton, page 2

EXPERIENCE

Norwood Car Supply, Inc.

Financial Consultant/Accounting Manager

Handled cost and budget reporting and automated accounting services for company doing $2 million in annual sales. Supervised two accountants.

Portland School Employees Federal Credit Union

Vice President, Accounting

Operated accounting system and supervised accounting staff for credit union with assets of $100 million.

Oregon National Bank and Trust

Designed and implemented cost and profit planning system and managed accounting system for bank with assets of $2.5 billion. Supervised accounting staff, prepared financial reports, filed corporate income taxes, planned and implemented branch expansion.

Compliance Officer

Controller

Cost Accountant

EDUCATION

B.S. in Business Administration, Washington State University

Networking Resume Sample   **HEALTH CARE**

Situation: Has over twenty years in traditional medicine/dentistry.

Job he wants: To move to a profession where he can practice alternative health care and utilize strong interest in education, nutrition and other forms of alternative health care.

LOWELL CHANEY
115 E. 72nd Street
New York, New York 10021
(212) 799-2222

(Don't necessarily need an objective, but once you're more focused, it would be wise.)

PERSONAL AND PROFESSIONAL INTERESTS

A compassionate and committed professional with a wealth of experience in the field of oral medicine and broad knowledge in nutrition, physical exercise and alternative forms of medicine.

Strong interest in ecology and contributing to the education of others' health and physical and emotional well-being. Desire to utilize abilities to relate well to diverse group of people, communicate with enthusiasm and plan and organize projects.

Extensive self-study and exposure to:

- Acupuncture and acupressure
- Biofeedback
- Homeopathy
- Kinesiology
- Massage therapy and shiatsu massage
- Stress management
- Meditation, yoga, tai chi and aikido
- Exercise programs including aerobics, weight training, bulk building, weight loss, injury prevention
- Sports including biking, running, swimming, scuba diving, racquetball, squash, soccer, tennis, hiking
- Nutrition including vitamins, vegetarianism, macrobiotics, metabolism

SELECTED ACHIEVEMENTS RELATED TO HEALTH EDUCATION

- Evaluated 42-year-old male who was overweight and depressed; established program that included regimented exercise, new diet and counseling that led to considerable weight loss and happier relationships.

- Educated 45-year-old woman who was overweight and malcontent on the value of physical exercise and balanced diet through demonstration of exercise, introduction to massage therapy and development of new diet; result was well-balanced, healthier person and avid horsewoman.

- Modeled strict vegetarian diet and physical exercise program for 50-year-old male who hadn't exercised in 20 years and had poor eating habits; result was substantial weight loss and avid skier and scuba diver.

PROFESSIONAL EXPERIENCE

MEDICAL:

Family Practice Dentist, New York, New York   1973-Present
Develop and manage practice that treats up to 2,500 patients. Includes cosmetic and implant dentistry and nutritional counseling. Supervise eight staff members.

TEACHING/TRAINING:

Instructor, New York University, College of Dentistry, New York, New York 1978-1979
Taught practice management to senior dental students.

Trainer, McPeep Associates, New York, New York   1975
Taught process of administering nitrous oxide analgesia to dentists for dental equipment distributor.

EDUCATION

D.D.S. The Ohio State University, College of Dentistry 1973

600 Hours Post Graduate Courses in Dentistry

Graduate Studies in Psychology, New York University

Private Yoga Classes and Tai Chi Training

HUMAN RESOURCES/COMMUNICATIONS

Situation: Recent experience in nonprofit and government in management and public relations roles. Earlier experience in human resources and communications.
Job she wants: Human resources and/or communications.

LILIANN P. ACKERMAN
2009 Marion Parkway
St. Louis, Missouri 63139
Home: (314) 644-2222   Office: (314) 642-2222

PROFILE

Fifteen years of record accomplishments in manufacturing, nonprofit and government organizations. Persuasive leader who balances human and capital resources to achieve bottom-line results. Known for ability to garner support from others and foster an environment of teamwork and accomplishment. Expertise encompasses:

- Media relations
- Public speaking
- Special event planning
- Budgeting and financial management
- Training
- Speech writing
- Personnel and organizational development
- Marketing communications including development of videos, brochures and newsletters
- Planning corporate reorganization and downsizing
- Strategic planning to define and implement corporate goals and objectives
- Lobbying state and local government for public issues and private industry concerns

EXPERIENCE

Director
St. Louis Chamber of Commerce, St. Louis, Missouri   1992-Present
Direct operations and activities that serve 1,200 members comprised of corporate executives, government and board of education professionals. Oversee press relations and communications for special projects. Serve on boards of directors of local and regional organizations. Edit and publish monthly newsletter.
- Initiated aggressive telemarketing and promotional campaign that increased membership by 35% and revenues by 23% in highly competitive market.
- Directed ongoing lobbying program to state legislators and administrators that resulted in state commitment to build $150 million regional highway.
- Conducted fundraising campaign to establish new holiday lighting program for downtown, resulting in individual and corporate contributions of over $200,000.
- Developed marketing campaign for annual golf tournament/fundraiser that increased profits 500%.

Human Resource Director

<u>Regis Lee Metal Company</u>, Licking, Missouri   1987-1992

Directed human resource and public relations functions for 1,200-employee, metal stamping and assemblies manufacturer. Coordinated quality assurance training for management and line workers. Managed apprenticeship program for tool and die makers. Designed and presented orientation programs. Represented company on boards of local and regional organizations.

- Initiated recruitment program that expanded personnel by 33% during 18-month period of major growth for company.
- Organized and coordinated United Way program that increased donations 200%.
- Trained management and staff of diverse workforce on multicultural issues; program became benchmark for diversity training in major U.S. corporations.

Associate Director/Communications Manager

<u>Missouri Development Council</u>, St. Louis, Missouri   1982-1986

Directed $8 million Job Training Partnership Program in 12 counties in central Missouri. Designed and oversaw training programs for area businesses, emphasizing industrial start-up training and working closely with local and state government officials. Developed proposals to induce companies to locate plants and offices in area. Organized press conferences and handled media relations.

EDUCATION

B.A. Public Administration 1982
Northern Kentucky University

Self-taught personal computer skills including spreadsheets, desktop publishing, word processing, databases.

MANAGEMENT

Situation: Has been in sales, management and marketing.
Job he wants: Management position in which he focuses solely on Hispanic population.

JUAN DONITAS
6767 Wayward Place
Longboat Key, Florida 34227
Home: (813) 382-2222   E-Mail: donjuan@com.com

OBJECTIVE

Position of significant responsibility that utilizes broad range of management abilities, sales, training and marketing background and thorough understanding of Hispanic market. Qualified by ability to quickly develop rapport and work well with a diverse group of people, communicate with enthusiasm, motivate others to meet goals and objectives and speak fluent English and Spanish.

Known for open-door management style that leads to cohesive teams and increased productivity with expertise in:
- Operations
- Customer service
- Personnel functions
- Profit and loss
- Sales techniques

Summarizes and emphasizes experience that relates to goal

EXPERIENCE

Abe Lincoln National Insurance, Lakeland, Florida   1990-Present

Manager, Home Office Accounts   1994-Present
Oversee development of new department that will serve 150,000 customers. Handle strategic planning, recruiting, hiring and training. Establish operating procedures. Act as liaison between field and home office.

Proof of his efforts

- Trained 35 new sales representatives in English and Spanish in effective sales techniques and product information; participants reported confidence in working in Hispanic and non-Hispanic markets.
- Motivated sales staff to take initiative to work more closely with customers that saved accounts worth $56 million.
- Recruited and hired ten sales managers that allowed company to expand into Hispanic market representing 20% of population.
- Created and presented training for new African-American employees that facilitated understanding of corporate culture and significantly hastened acclimation time.

Juan Donitas, page 2

Marketing Assistant/Sales Associate   1990-1993
Handled marketing effort to develop business in Hispanic market. Designed and produced brochures in Spanish. Recruited and trained sales managers in predominately Spanish-speaking geographical areas. Analyzed market research. Oversaw three-state sales territory.

Bilingua Language School, Miami, Florida   1989
Spanish Teacher/Translator
Taught Spanish to adults at various proficiency levels in group setting and one-on-one. Acted as simultaneous translator for Fortune 500 company and U.S. federal court system.

Brunswick Shoes, Boston, Massachusetts   1988
Marketing Intern
Created and executed marketing plan targeted at Hispanic market in Miami, Florida.

EDUCATION

B.S. in Marketing and Management, Northwestern University 1989
Chosen to attend IBM Marketing Seminar in Puerto Rico 1987

MANUFACTURING OPERATIONS

Situation: Job titles have been in quality assurance, although some of his experience is in overall operations.
Job he wants: Broader scope of responsibility in operations position.

MOY MING
5858 Pickerington Road
San Diego, California 92127
(619) 592-2222

OBJECTIVE
Operations position in company seeking a leader who can contribute in a team environment to overall profitability.

SUMMARY OF QUALIFICATIONS
Tenacious, results-oriented professional with hands-on experience in new product development, information systems and quality. Known as an astute troubleshooter with the ability to analyze and design efficient internal systems.

Proven strengths to:
- Clearly communicate goals and objectives
- Envision and implement operational strategies
- Analyze and systematize processes and procedures
- Apply in-depth computer knowledge and create software

Important skills to emphasize

Emphasizes overall knowledge

Broad knowledge of:

- All facets of manufacturing operations, personnel management and new business ventures
- Petro chemical products
- Raw materials, standards, analytical tests, equipment, blending processes
- Chemical reactivities and flammabilities
- EPA and OSHA regulations regarding chemical spills, labeling, permits, standards, transportation
- NAFTA regulations
- Quality systems including customer surveys, control charts, statistical process control, auditing
- ISO9001 quality system standard
- Hazardous material reporting systems
- Imports/Exports

ACHIEVEMENTS
- Oversaw development and implementation of quality system surveys, on-site audits and delivery performance reports that enhanced communication with suppliers and reduced shipments that didn't conform to quality standards by 95%.

Moy Ming, page 2

*Examples of how he's affected
whole company's success*

- Developed and conducted training for staff and management on quality improvement tools and led troubleshooting meetings that raised manufacturing process conformance ratings from 65% to 95%.

- Led team in writing standardized procedures for company operations, including production, maintenance, customer service, finance, research and development and quality, raising profile of company as having the best quality systems in industry and increasing new business by 200%.

- Created highly complex database software system to generate MSDS documentation for formulated products that reduced preparation time from 3 hours to 10 minutes and error rate from 75% to 2%.

- Wrote software to automate analytical instruments that doubled number of analyses performed in one day.

- Reorganized purchasing system for more efficient scheduling and cost monitoring that saved company 2% in annual operating costs.

- Designed new information system that created cohesive system for tracking material and customer criteria; increased customer satisfaction 50% and business by 20% without adding staff.

- Developed customized software that greatly enhanced quality control and streamlined purchasing and formulation processes, created EPA reports and labels and aided production scheduling, saving company $250,000 in software costs first year.

EXPERIENCE

<u>Nina Pinta Manufacturing</u>, San Diego, CA   1990-Present

Director of Quality   1992-Present
Lead development of quality systems and productivity improvement in operations and product development for manufacturer and distributor of lubricants, industrial metalworking and fluids and fuels. Create and implement information system strategies. Interpret regulatory and hazard requirements of certifying boards. Develop standard operating procedures. Perform internal and external quality system audits.

Manager of Quality Control   1990-1992
Develop analytical methods and perform testing on products, raw materials and field samples. Maintain records and report analytical data. Assist research department to systematically evaluate and develop new products.

Moy Ming, page 3

<u>C & M Research/Chemical</u>, San Diego, CA   1987-1990

Research Chemist
Develop chemical laboratory procedures and analytical methods for manufacturer and distributor of engine oils and refined petroleum products. Formulate industrial lubricating products. Develop software that automated analytical instrumentation, calculating results and modeling product yield.

EDUCATION

M.B.A. Quantitative Methods, University of California at San Diego 1987

B.S. Chemistry, Massachusetts Institute of Technology 1984

PROFESSIONAL AFFILIATIONS

American Society for Quality Control
U.S. Chemical Society
Society for Professional Managers

MARKETING

Situation: All experience in banking as coordinator and marketer of special programs. Only four years of actual work experience.
Job she wants: Marketing position that utilizes strong background and knowledge of senior citizen market.

BARBARA STREISTAR
9012 Derby Drive
Austin, Texas 78733
(512) 467-2222

OBJECTIVE

Good to use objective since she's so focused

Marketing position that utilizes strong background and knowledge of senior citizen market and contributes to the building of long-lasting relationships.

SUMMARY OF QUALIFICATIONS

Responsible, marketing-oriented professional with eight years' educational and hands-on experience in business and marketing and proven skills to:

- Work well with diverse groups of people
- Clearly communicate ideas and concepts
- Inspire others to take action
- Create marketing programs and strategies, goals and objectives
- Organize special events and procedures
- Manage people and projects

Thorough knowledge of senior citizen market. Known for ability to think clearly, work independently and be a creative problem solver. Demonstrated success in:

- Customer relations
- Promotion including newsletters and advertising
- Media relations
- Travel and special event coordination
- Public speaking
- Management
- Development

EXPERIENCE

Second National Bank, Austin, Texas   1993-Present

Senior Club Manager   1994-Present

Emphasizes senior market knowledge
Oversee marketing and management of Banking Center locations in three retirement communities. Manage staff of five. Analyze profitability of each banking center. Handle personnel functions including hiring and performance evaluations. Plan and coordinate open houses and promotional seminars targeted to retirement community residents and families. Liaison between bank management and retirement centers.

- Manage and oversee marketing senior citizen checking account and lifestyle program representing 25% of bank's checking accounts.

Results

Barbara Streistar, page 2

<u>**Senior Club Coordinator**</u>   1993-1994
Developed marketing strategies for senior citizen checking account and lifestyle program serving over 100,000 members including coordination of education seminars,
travel programs and community sponsored activities. Hosted and facilitated tours,
seminars and travel. Cultivated relationships with members. Worked closely with
bank departments and senior management. Gave presentations to senior centers,
bank employees and public. Wrote monthly newsletter.

Results   • Developed and coordinated promotional program that more than doubled
checking deposits over two years.

<u>Internships and employment in school:</u>

<u>**Research Coordinator**</u>, **Marriott Research**, Austin, Texas   1989

<u>**Marketing Intern**</u>, **Austin Regional Transit Authority**, Austin, Texas   1988
Assisted with new signage promotional program. Compiled demographic and geographic profiles.

EDUCATION

B.A. Management
Texas A & M University 1990

Ohio State University
Division of International Studies Programs Abroad London, England 1987

ACTIVITIES

Member, Heart Association Fundraising Young Professional Committee, 1993
Member, Seniors Masterworks Art Show Committee, 1994, 1995
Member, Area Agency on Aging

*Shows more interest
in seniors*

MARKETING

Situation: All her experience is at a large company.
Job she wants: Marketing in small, entrepreneurial firm.

DANIELLE PERRY
4556 Ripple Road
Milwaukee, Wisconsin 43213
(414) 332-2222

OBJECTIVE

Marketing

A leadership position in an entrepreneurial company that results in increased profit and market share and utilizes proven strengths to:
- Lead teams from concept development to implementation
- Envision marketing strategies and new products
- Solve budget and marketing problems
- Communicate ideas and results with clarity and focus

QUALIFICATIONS

Entrepreneurs value this

A creative and resourceful problem solver with six years in product development with emphasis on strategic planning in Fortune 100 consumer products manufacturer. Reputation for innovative approaches and willingness to take risks. Influential in helping others meet goals and objectives through creative problem solving. *Entrepreneurs value these*
- Understanding of global market, consumer practices, supplier relations
- Expertise in advertising, group presentations, training
- Versed in quantitative and qualitative research
- Extensive experience with multifunctional and multicultural teams
- Speak Japanese, French and Hebrew

ACHIEVEMENTS

- Led teams of creative and technical staff to develop marketing strategies for new products that increased sales by 75%.

- Managed project that measured appeal and feasibility of introducing foreign snack food brand to U.S. market, saving company $10 million.

- Instrumental in establishing Web page on Internet for leading skin care product that will supplement conventional consumer comment phone lines.

- Championed innovative research tool that quantitatively measures product appeal.

EXPERIENCE

Lictor & Lace, Milwaukee, Wisconsin   1991-1997

Project Marketing Manager, Skin Care Division   1994-1997
Oversee concept development of new products for $4 billion division in global Fortune 100 consumer products manufacturer. Lead teams of technical and creative staff in Europe and North America to create new product ideas and marketing strategies. Facilitate brainstorming sessions.

Associate, Product Research, Beauty Aides Division   1991-1994
Conducted research on consumer habits, product formulation and new product formulas. Wrote documentation to support advertising claims.

Andrew Jergens Company, Cincinnati, Ohio   1990
Intern, Marketing Sector
Handled data entry, compiled statistical reports and worked closely with sales and marketing research staff to develop management reports.

EDUCATION

B.A. in Marketing Indiana University 1990
Continuing education includes: Seven Habits of Highly Successful People, New Product Development . . . Leading Others Through Visioning

MARKETING COMMUNICATION

> *Situation*: Most recent experience is for the federal government, and she had a tough time demonstrating how it translated into the business world.
> *Job she wants*: Marketing communications in a public or nonprofit organization.

MARLENA BETRICH
119922 Longmeadow Drive
Arlington, Virginia 22208
(703) 276-2222

OBJECTIVE

Position that requires extensive experience in strategic planning and marketing communications to enhance a company's image and visibility, promote services and products and achieve overall strategic goals by using strengths to:
- Analyze communication needs
- Plan marketing communication programs
- Conceptualize and implement projects
- Organize and manage complex or sensitive projects and information
- Articulate benefits of a product or service

QUALIFICATIONS

Innovative marketer with 18 years' experience in integrated business communications and strategic marketing. Specific expertise includes:

- Strategic plans
- Corporate communication
- Sales support materials
- Advertising
- Direct mail
- Media relations
- Trade shows/special events
- Speech writing
- Script writing
- Proposal development
- Editing
- Managing creative services

ACCOMPLISHMENTS

- Spearheaded corporate strategic planning, external communication and marketing support programs that allowed company to achieve 100% increase in revenue despite severe market downturn.

  — Bottom-line results

- Conducted market research, developed marketing procedures and trained management consultants for Big 6 accounting firm to sell services to untapped market with multimillion dollars in sales potential.

- Initiated sales support program that explained benefits of complex, high-tech telecommunications services to customers in simple language, reducing perceived risk of buying from nontraditional source.

  Understands public relations —

- Conceptualized and produced print advertising campaign and integrated marketing support materials for company that had received negative media attention, significantly improving perception of services in the marketplace.

  — Understands public relations

Marlena Betrich, page 2

• Played key creative role in developing multimedia training packages that allowed major educational publisher to penetrate business market.
• Instrumental in developing visibility for minority company that altered perception of firm as start-up operation to a recognized player in industry.

Putting job titles first
emphasizes job functions

EXPERIENCE

Director, Corporate Strategic Planning and Communication   1988-1993
Magnuson, Incorporated, Washington, DC
Established and directed strategic planning, external communication and marketing support functions for $15 million technical services/custom manufacturing contractor serving federal government and commercial customers.

Marketing Coordinator   1987-1988
Liggett & Foster Federal Management Consulting Services, Arlington, VA
Organized marketing effort for partners in division of Big 6 accounting firm to establish management consulting practice serving the federal government.

Manager, Corporate Communication   1985-1987
Program Manager, Communication, Training Division   1983-1985
St. Paul Systems, Arlington, VA
Handled corporate communications for technical services contractor serving federal government.

Communication Consultant   1982-1983
Washington, DC
Provided writing, editing and production services to associations, businesses and public agencies. Conceptualized and managed development of print materials and audiovisual presentations such as safety belt campaign for federal government, patient information materials for medical association and educational film for major passenger carrier.

Director, Communication and Public Affairs   1978-1981
The Northwest Institute, Washington, DC
Established communication function to support customers and internal needs of management consulting/training firm specializing in Native American affairs.

Manager, Membership Information Services   1977-1978
The Brick Association, Washington, DC
Managed development of brochures, directories, newsletters and press releases for national association serving 88 member companies. Supervised editorial and production staff.

Marketing Media Specialist   1976-1977
RDG Telecommunications Corporation, Washington, DC
Developed company's first strategic communication program to market voice-data communication services to large commercial customers.

EDUCATION

B.A., Marketing University of Hawaii 1973
Seminars: Corporate Ethics in Professional Services Industry, Strategic Planning for Small Companies

PROJECT MANAGEMENT

Situation: Has a varied background in project management, cost analysis and supervision.
Job he wants: Project management.

CHARLES DUVALL
12 Liberty Lane
Melville, New York 17488
(516) 423-2222

Emphasizes project management early on

OBJECTIVE
Position that builds upon extensive experience in project management and expertise in cost analysis and supervision and requires proven abilities to:
- Analyze accounting processes and job functions to create efficient operations
- Collaborate and act as liaison between staff and management to meet common goals
- Communicate procedures and objectives
- Coordinate schedules and workload to meet deadlines

QUALIFICATIONS
Great experience to support his objective

A dedicated professional with a reputation for building teams to ensure timely, accurate and quality completion of projects. Possesses a broad range of expertise in increasingly responsible positions including direct involvement in accounting, purchasing and operations.

Successful track record and knowledge in:
- Proposals and contracts
- Contract administration
- Accounts payable, cost accounting, budgets
- Purchase orders and work orders
- Inventory
- Blueprint reading and drafting techniques
- Team building and leadership
- Management
- Personal and mainframe computers
- Training
- Estimating
- Vendor relations
- Construction industry including field inspections, regulatory issues, analysis of labor and material costs

EXPERIENCE

<u>Lakeland Gas & Electric Company</u>   1965-1992

Accounting/Engineering Analyst   1976-1992
Managed accounting and engineering functions associated with project management for complex construction projects ranging from $5 million to over $600 million. Analyzed and determined labor, material and overhead costs; prepared detailed cost reports and sketches. Planned, coordinated and scheduled field inspections. Handled purchasing function including vendors, bills of materials, contracts and purchase orders. Prepared documentation and oversaw regulatory inquiries. Managed three staff members.

- Converted antiquated IBM card cost control system to online system that increased retrieval time by 70% and dramatically increased management's control over project and spending.
- Developed new purchase order system that increased efficiency of routing, accounts payable and accounting systems by 30%.
- Facilitated team building and leadership program that developed and implemented new performance review system; resulted in creation of uniform measurement tool for all management employees.
- Awarded Team Spirit Award in 1989 for successfully meeting deadline of multimillion dollar project.
- Awarded Outstanding Performance Award for participation in development of new performance review system.

Draftsman   1965-1975
Responsible for creative design and drafting of architectural, civil and structural projects. Estimated materials, staff time and costs. Taught drafting, design and use of computer-aided systems to draftspeople.

EDUCATION

B.S. Administrative Management New York University 1978
A.S. Information Processing Systems New York University 1976

Received degrees while working full-time.

Continuing education includes classes in:
Personal Computers, Lotus 1-2-3, WordPerfect 5.1, DOS, Stress Management, Problem Solving

PUBLIC RELATIONS

Situation: Background in marketing/sales and public relations and nonprofit.
Job he wants: Public relations leadership position in multicultural, nonprofit environment.

DAKOTA INESCO
7117 Penzias Way
San Jose, California 95123
(408) 265-2222

SUMMARY

A resourceful, results-oriented team player with a wealth of experience in advertising, media relations and public relations in corporate and nonprofit environments. Known for ability to see the big picture, lead with consistency and fairness and get things done on time with limited resources.
- Innovative leader with sound business judgment
- Committed to helping others achieve goals and objectives
- Strong interest and exposure to multicultural issues and diversity
Knowledge encompasses:
- Management
- Sales and strategic marketing
- Public speaking
- Training
- Trade shows and exhibits
- Newsletter and brochure design
- Television production
- Grant and proposal writing
- Media and community relations
- Fund-raising

ACHIEVEMENTS
- Presented benefits and features of leading edge office technology at national press conferences that resulted in stories in *The New York Times*, *The Wall Street Journal* and dozens of major trade journals.

- Contributed to leading team of marketing specialists to meet annual sales goals; exceeded goal by 100%.

- Acted as liaison between technically minded product managers and advertising agency, culminating in marketing plan that encompassed sound strategy and technical features of products.

- Planned and promoted special events resulting in record attendance, that included seminars for teens and women on issues ranging from multicultural understanding to self-esteem.

- Initiated and created monthly teleconferences that included interviews with product managers and led to an informed and motivated sales force across the U.S. and Canada.

- Planned and oversaw trade show exhibits and acted as media spokesperson for major conferences across the U.S.

Dakota Inesco, page 2

EXPERIENCE

NONPROFIT: *List first to emphasize nonprofit experience*

California Outreach Advisory Board, San Jose, California   1993-1996
Outreach Consultant and Community Liaison

Multi-cultural experience

- Raised funds and led restructuring of Laotian-American organization serving Vietnamese community. Wrote successful grant proposal to state's Office of Refugees and Immigrants. Raised funds and designed and implemented anti-domestic violence campaign for Cambodian Mutual Assistance Association that reached 15,000 Cambodians in their native language.
- Planned and coordinated workshops for women on self-esteem and sexism.
- Developed and presented esteem building and conflict resolution training to inner-city children. Worked with teachers, social worker and principal on behavior modification. Increased parent involvement in Child Assault Prevention Program.

MARKETING/SALES AND PUBLIC RELATIONS:

Decimal Savings & Investment, Inc., San Jose, California   1981-1993
Advertising Specialist, Marketing Division   1990-1993
Oversaw $20 million advertising budget for third largest financial services firm in U.S. Reviewed creative concepts and media schedules. Managed trade shows. Guided production of radio, TV and print ads.

Marketing/Public Relations Specialist, Marketing Division   1987-1990
Developed and implemented marketing programs for financial services, banking and brokerage products. Supported field sales organization with product information. Managed and coordinated internal marketing communications. Planned trade shows.
Organized press conferences and worked closely with media.   *Public relations*

Product Marketing Associate   1981-1987
Developed intial product position and sales and marketing strategies.

Digital Corporation, San Francisco, California   1977-1980
Senior Sales Representative
Sold high-speed, computer printing systems to key decision makers in medium and large companies. Achieved "Rookie of the Year" at 130% of quota.

EDUCATION
M.B.A. University of California Berkeley 1980
B.A. Business Administration Santa Monica College 1977

COMMUNITY ACTIVITIES

Jaycees, Youth at Risk Program, San Francisco   *Multi-cultural experience*
Volunteer, Crisis Hotline
Coordinated programs for disabled and hearing impaired

REAL ESTATE APPRAISAL

> *Situation*: He's had many positions that don't support his objective.
> *Job he wants*: Real Estate Appraisal.

MELVIN BROOKS
5666 Santos Way
Columbus, Ohio 43216
(614) 228-2222

OBJECTIVE: REAL ESTATE APPRAISAL

Position that will build upon extensive interest in real estate and property valuation and experience and education in the field of real estate appraisal.

QUALIFICATIONS

A responsible, hard-working professional known for attention to detail, accuracy, thoroughness and seeing a project through to completion.

Education includes:
Completion of 75-hour Real Estate Appraisal courses required for Ohio licensing
Real Estate Appraisal Courses Columbus Technical College 1995
B.A. Drawing Columbus College of Art and Design 1988

Specific skills include:
• Illustrations, renderings and basic engineering and schematic drawing
• Map and blueprint reading
• Property inspection
• Ability to interpret and utilize plat and street maps
• Strong skill in articulating ideas and concepts
• Usage of video camera

— Emphasizes experience related to objective

RELATED EXPERIENCE

Parinelli & Associates, Columbus, Ohio   1994-Present
Field Technician
Inspect property to determine compliance with federal mandates for architectural and engineering consulting firm.

Pintas Appraising Service, Columbus, Ohio   1990-1994
Videographer   1992-1994
Videotaped thousands of buildings and residential properties to update records for Franklin County Auditor's Office for company providing real estate appraisal and related services to county governments.

Melvin Brooks, page 2

Emphasizes experience related to objective

Residential Data Collector   1990-1992

Analyzed and inspected residential real estate to determine accuracy of county records, ascertain property improvements and verify dimensions of house and attachments. Interviewed property owners and verified building permits.

Freelance Illustrator and Designer   1990-Present
- Renderings of homes for real estate agents
- Greater Columbus Jaycees: Assist in remodeling of booth facade for Ohio State Fair
- Oversee design projects for Columbus Chapter of Heart Association

OTHER EXPERIENCE:

Emphasizes his "visual" expertise

K & B Associates, Columbus, Ohio   1988-Present
Tax Preparer
Prepare individual tax returns. Work one-on-one with clients.

Costumes, Inc., Columbus, Ohio   1988-1990
Production Assistant
Oversaw final preparation of costumes for company that produces character costumes. Handled packaging and shipping of products. Worked extensively with synthetic materials and power tools.

The P & L Company, Columbus, Ohio   1987
Accounting Clerk
Tabulated information and verified records for temporary project through Manpower, Inc.

COMMUNITY ACTIVITIES

- Coordinator, Monitor Program, Columbus Artists Group Effort 1987
- Installation setup, Columbus Art Gallery 1985
- Volunteer for Jaycees, Art for Columbus Conference

Potential liability: Older worker.   **RETAIL OPERATIONS**

ANGELA MAXIMILIAN
818 Lillith Road
Boston, Massachusetts 02116
(517) 437-2222

OBJECTIVE

Operations
A position of significant responsibility that requires general management, operations and financial control experience along with strong training, problem solving and computer skills.

QUALIFICATIONS

A highly organized, take-charge professional with extensive experience in operations management in positions of increasing responsibility with a Fortune 500 company and a proven track record in the following areas:

- Sales management
- Budget, planning and expense control
- Sales forecasting
- Customer service
- Scheduling
- Training and development
- Operations analysis and decision making
- Human resources
- Compensation and benefit administration
- Merchandising
- Marketing
- Inventory
- Interior construction and renovation
- Vendor negotiations
- Business planning
- Lotus 1-2-3, WordPerfect

ACCOMPLISHMENTS

- Turned around unprofitable $12 million operation, increasing profitability by $650,000 by implementing aggressive cost reductions, developing sales training program and creating coaching environment that emphasized teamwork.

- Analyzed and redesigned telecommunications system that enhanced efficiency of operation and reduced overall expense by 15%.

- Originated plan that reduced inventory shrinkage by 38%.

- Developed computerized training program that modeled accounting system and resulted in staff's thorough understanding of cause and effect, significantly contributing to increased profitability.

- Presented ongoing training to supervisors and management on empowerment, sales techniques, situational management and teamwork.

- Created proforma income and financial statements that determined most cost-effective methods and financial payback for remodeling and expansion projects.

Angela Maximilian, page 2

- Developed innovative marketing techniques that expanded customer base and increased sales volume.

- Maintained smooth flow of operations during remodeling of 115,000 square foot facility over five-month period.

- Expanded sales of high profit margin services, improving profitability by 30%.

EXPERIENCE

L-Mart, Inc.   *Only lists relevant experience*   1970-1993

General Manager, Lowell, Massachusetts   1989-1993
Directed operations of $33 million retail facility including management of 215 employees. Planned and implemented staff training. Full profit and loss responsibility.

General Manager, Newark, New Jersey   1987-1989
Oversaw daily operations of $18 million retail facility including management of 115 employees and full responsibility for profit and loss. Managed remodeling project for 20,000 square foot operation.

Operating & Sales Promotion Manager, Plymouth, Massachusetts   1978-1984
Managed apparel and home fashion departments for $15 million operation. Negotiated contracts with outside vendors. Managed advertising function. Active in community relations including teaching business class to junior high students.

Human Resource Manager, Arlington, Virginia   1976-1978
Managed human resource function for 1,000 employees serving five locations including warehouse, service department, credit/collection department and three retail operations. Built strong community alliance through activities in local business group, chamber of commerce and schools including student co-op program.

Assistant Store Manager, Arlington, Virginia   1975-1976
Supervised and managed relocation of $2 million retail operation.

Management Trainee Program, Lowell, Massachusetts   1970-1971

EDUCATION

No graduation date to play down age

B.A., Marketing, Boston University

RETAIL SALES

> *Situation*: Older worker who had been in senior management.
> *Job she wants*: Staff position in customer service in retail, preferably selling building materials or something related.

FULTON CHANEL

98211 Hastings Avenue • **Palatine, Illinois 60067** • **(708) 202-2222**

OBJECTIVE

— Good since she's so focused

A position in customer service in retail that builds on extensive knowledge of building and manufacturing materials.

PROFILE

— Plays up customer service

A mature and results-oriented problem solver with a talent for building goodwill, a reputation for getting the job done and vast knowledge of daily operations of a business.

Strong interest in contributing experience and talents to a business that values its customers and seeks ways to build customer loyalty while delivering high quality service. Expertise includes:

- Manufacturing, mechanical and production processes
- Scheduling
- Pricing

- Negotiations
- Sourcing
- Variety of building and manufacturing materials

Supports objective

EXPERIENCE

Horowitz & Leonard Shoes, Chicago, Illinois   1970-1995
Vice President, New Product Development
Oversaw development of new product lines. Worked closely with sales and factory personnel to ensure quality. Researched raw materials and presented concepts and costs to management and sales force.

Director, New Product Development
Oversaw new product development for three regions in U.S.

Manager, New Product Development
Managed new product development process for Midwest region.

— Downplays senior management experience

EDUCATION

B.A., University of North Carolina

INTERESTS

— Supports objective

- Avid home remodeler
- Member, Chicago Rehab Association
- Tour Guide, Homearama 1994-Present

TECHNICAL SUPPORT AND SERVICE

> *Situation*: Has been a repair technician, remodeler and maintenance supervisor.
> *Job he wants*: Technical support position.

WALDO LUCKWORTH
6789 Morrow Avenue
Cleveland, Ohio 44116
(216) 431-2222

OBJECTIVE

Technical support position for a manufacturer of operational equipment that utilizes vast experience and knowledge in electronics, mechanics and refrigeration.

QUALIFICATIONS

A diplomatic, efficient-minded service technician with 14 years in supervision and repair and maintenance of buildings, equipment, electrical and operational systems, with a reputation for being resourceful in handling emergencies and deadlines. Specific expertise includes:

- Thorough knowledge of maintenance and repair of HVAC systems
- Customer service
- Inventory control
- Purchasing
- Troubleshooting
- Scheduling
- Preventative maintenance
- Certified HVAC Training

- Remodeling skills including: roofing, masonry, woodworking, tiling, drywall, rewiring electrical systems, plumbing

EXPERIENCE

Independent Repair Technician and Remodeler   1995-Present
Projects include maintenance and operation of AC systems; residential remodeling.

London Falling Properties, Cleveland, OH   1990-1995
Maintenance Supervisor
Oversaw maintenance, repair and purchasing of supplies for 450 apartment units. Supervised staff of five. Daily contact with tenants and suppliers. Projects included maintenance and operation of AC systems and residential remodeling. ◄—— *Can deal with customers*
- By contributing skills and knowledge in HVAC, totally eliminated outside contractors, saving company $25,000 annually.

Waldo Luckworth, page 2

Martin Wade Properties, Warren, OH   1988-1990
<u>Maintenance Supervisor</u>
Handled maintenance of 250 apartment units, including painting, drywall, repair, plumbing, electrical, HVAC repair, carpentry, preventative maintenance. Supervised staff of three.

Results

- Repaired outdated boiler system from 1940s that saved company $40,000 for new heating system.
- Developed proposal for installation of more efficient heating system that paid for itself through savings in heating bills over eight years.

Harvard Green Apartments, Chillicothe, OH   1986-1988
Manager/Service Technician of 80-unit apartment complex.

Clinton Park Apartments, Chillicothe, OH   1983-1986
Service Technician for 400-unit apartment complex.

More results

- Oversaw process of repairing and remodeling vacant apartments, reducing vacancy rate by 50% within two months.
- Devised and implemented inventory control system that virtually eliminated waiting time for parts and supplies and dramatically increased efficiency of maintenance process.

EDUCATION

Certified Apartment Maintenance Technician   1990
National Apartment Association

Continuing education classes include coursework at Cleveland Technical College, Oaks Vocational School, Ohio College of Applied Sciences 1973-1988

TRAINING

> *Situation*: Half of his experience is in sales.
> *Job he wants*: To be a technical trainer.

LARAMY IRONS
1112 Pundent Street
Princeton, New Jersey 08541
(908) 249-2222

OBJECTIVE: Technical Training

Quickly emphasizes training skills

To utilize experience in electronic publishing and presentations, media integration, sales and training and proven strengths to:
• Research and translate technical information into understandable language
• Present complex concepts to nontechnical audiences
• Coordinate and organize multiple projects

He knows his material

Qualified by nine years' sales and training in the personal computer industry and extensive knowledge in the usage and application of personal computers.
Expertise includes ability to:
• Use Macintosh computers and related third party products
• Develop and present Macintosh training and presentations
• Present new product information
• Respond quickly to changing market conditions and products
• Understand graphic and print production processes

Proficient in:
Adobe PageMaker 6.0, Adobe Persuasion 3.0, Macromedia FreeHand 5.5, System 7.5, Microsoft Works 4.0, Adobe Type Manager 3.9, Fractal Design Painter 4.0, Microsoft Excel 5.0, FileMaker Pro 3.0, Macromedia Director 5.0, Adobe Streamline 3.1, Adobe Photoshop 3.0, QuarkXPress 3.32, Adobe Acrobat 3.0, Adobe PageMill 2.0 and Adobe SiteMill 1.0.

EXPERIENCE

Trainer/Sales Associate   1992-1996
Orange Computer, Inc., New Rochelle, New York
Developed and delivered training to customers, staff and management on electronic publishing and media integration for Macintosh for manufacturer of computer equipment and software development firm. Conducted sales, networking and communications training. Organized Macintosh and Orange II product events. Worked closely with sales representatives and management. Handled sales accounts for one region.

Has been recognized for his skills

• Established reputation as publishing specialist for region.
• Received Outstanding Trainer Award.
• Received Regional Impact Award for new product training.
• Developed manual to train department on use of new scanning system that resulted in cross-training of staff.

Account Executive   1988-1992
X-Tron Computers and X-Star Computers, New Rochelle, New York
Sold multiuser/multitasking computer systems, word processors and microcomputer systems to commercial businesses for distributors of computer hardware, a $5 million division of Comstar, manufacturer doing $12 million in sales. Gave group sales presentations and equipment demonstrations.
- Graduated second in class from Orange Training School.
- Sold over $1.5 million of equipment first three months.
- Named salesperson of the month.

EDUCATION

B.A. in Telecommunications, Kent State University 1988
Rayborn Electronic Publishing Seminars
Dale Carnegie courses on public speaking

ACTIVITIES

Member of Toastmasters

Resumes by Profession

ADMINISTRATION

CECILIA BANCROFT
7171 Elsinore Place
Spokane, Washington 99201
(509) 328-2222

SUMMARY OF QUALIFICATIONS

Resourceful and results-oriented executive with over twenty years in manufacturing in U.S. and international markets. Skilled liaison between management, sales and technical staff. Reputation for building trusting relationships.

Strengths include ability to research and analyze consumer trends and merchandising, plan projected sales and solve problems related to on-time delivery.

Expertise in:
- Negotiations
- Sourcing
- Production
- Scheduling
- Pricing

ACCOMPLISHMENTS

- Led management team to develop new source for manufacturing core footwear product. Negotiated long-term material and manufacturing needs, reducing costs and increasing profits by 10%.

- Conducted research through store buyers and consumers that enabled company to design and launch new products and grow division sales from $22 million to $56 million in four years.

- Initiated and developed expansion of company sourcing in Spain for value-priced footwear. Coordinated corporate and local factory efforts to meet production goals for new styles.

- Through negotiations and hands-on involvement, led team to expand product line that met customer needs; coordinated production in U.S., Spain and Korea.

- Coordinated purchasing, engineering and manufacturing functions to produce low cost, private label line of footwear that only used surplus materials and equipment.

EXPERIENCE

Epstein Shoes, Spokane, Washington   1975-1997

Vice President, Lunar Division   1990-1997
Oversaw development of new product lines for third largest U.S. shoe manufacturer. Worked closely with sales and factory personnel to ensure quality. Researched new materials and presented concepts and costs to management and sales force for division doing $55 million in business.

Cecilia Bancroft, page 2

Vice President, <u>Senora Division</u>   1985-1990
Managed new product development process for division doing $44 million in business.

Director Product Development, <u>International Division-Florence, Italy</u>   1975-1984
Oversaw new product development for division doing $52 million in business.

EDUCATION

B.A. Business University of Kansas

COMMUNITY AND RECOGNITION
• Chairperson, United Way Campaign 1991
• Who's Who Among American Businesswomen

ADMINISTRATION

BEATRICE LAMONT
32 West Circle Drive
Colorado Springs, Colorado 80956
(719) 544-2222

PROFILE

<u>Progressive leader</u> with consistent record of successfully leading complex organizations through change. Focused and committed to accomplishing goals.

<u>Superior skills</u> in strategic planning, creative problem solving, building consensus and achieving bottom-line results through teams.

<u>Expertise in</u> operations, accounting, planning, marketing and sales. In-depth understanding of industry trends, financial issues and impact of key decisions, regulatory affairs, unions and interest groups.

EXPERIENCE AND ACCOMPLISHMENTS

Denver Telecommunications   1973-Present

Senior Vice President   1992-Present
Develop and oversee overall and day-to-day operations, strategic planning and direction. Handle $100 million capital budget and $130 million operating income. Perform financial and operational analysis of company subsidiaries and recommend operational strategies.
- Championed plan to reduce capital expenditures by $15 million annually.
- Developed and implemented phases for reengineering of five divisions that saved $45 million.
- Created business plan that led to purchase of preferred shares by another corporation, creating $50 million cash to fund acquisition.
- Planned and implemented new strategic direction for four divisions that saved company average of $5.5 million annually.

Director, Regulatory Affairs   1989-1992
Oversaw government and regulatory affairs including regulatory proceedings, tariffs and pricing for regulated products and relationships with regulatory agencies.
- Initiated and gained approval for controversial rate plan that resulted in negotiated settlement and $13 million in rate increases during time of declining rates.
- Oversaw lobbying effort of regulatory agency that resulted in waiving rules that would cost $7 million in annual revenue.

Beatrice Lamont, page 2

Director, Operations 1985-1989

Oversaw operations of $750 million business.
- Spearheaded reengineering effort that resulted in annual savings of $6 million.
- Created task force to conduct financial and operational analysis of $150 million non-regulated business that went from $7 million loss to breaking even in six months.
- Formed quality teams and mandated training that turned around demoralized department into solution-oriented professionals.
- Oversaw joint venture worth $15 million.
- Managed divestiture of two subsidiaries.

Other positions include: 1973-1984

Manager: Planning and Operations Planning, Operations, Service, Plant Supervisor, Planning Supervisor.

EDUCATION

M.B.A. Colorado College 1979
B.S.B.A. Colgate University 1973

Continuing education includes Leadership to Win . . . Denver Center for Technical Education . . . Total Quality Management . . . Interactive Management

ACTIVITIES

- Colorado Telecommunications Association
- Colorado Political Action Committee
- Colorado Telecommunications Advisory Council, 1993-1994
- Jaycees Mentoring Program
- Board of Directors, School for Technical Training

RECOGNITION

- 1994 Colorado's Top Woman in Business

BOOKKEEPING

DENITA FLOSS
44 Refuse Way
Atlanta, Georgia 30307
(404) 893-9898

OBJECTIVE

Bookkeeping
Keep complete record of financial transactions and balance books in health care environment, using proven skills to:
- Systematize financial data
- Coordinate weekly, monthly and quarterly figures
- Keep business records orderly and up-to-date
- Research discrepancies
- Reconcile statements

QUALIFICATIONS

Highly organized, efficient and reliable professional offering ten years in bookkeeping and data entry with a reputation for getting the job done accurately. Proficient in WordPerfect 6.0, Lotus 1-2-3, Microsoft Word, Windows.

EXPERIENCE

Bookkeeper
<u>Lincoln Smith Insurance</u>, Atlanta, Georgia   1990-Present
Prepare billing and life insurance statements and reconcile statements for three branch offices. Handle data entry. Resolve invoice discrepancies between vendors and company.
- Researched discrepancies in money owed, saving company thousands of dollars in annual premiums.
- Entered yearly accounts receivable and payable of $10 million that resulted in detailed bimonthly trial balance sheet.

Accounting Clerk
<u>Barbados Health Group</u>, Atlanta, Georgia   1987-1990
Reconcile bank statements, prepare financial statements and accounts receivable and payable for distributors of lasers and related equipment for health care industry.
- Organized bank statements, trust funds and general checking accounts and developed ledgers that gave company trustees detailed monthly financial statements.
- Initiated and oversaw transfer of accounts payable system from home office to branch that cut processing time in half.

EDUCATION

Associates Degree in Arts and Sciences Atlanta Technical College 1982

MEMBERSHIPS

Southern States Bookkeepers Association

WILLIS BRUSETT
2300 Pennsylvania Street, Indianapolis, Indiana 46206   •   (317) 630-2222

SUMMARY

Engineering professional with broad-based experience in Computer Aided Engineering and demonstrated skills in team leadership with an emphasis on customer satisfaction.

Expertise in integrated engineering and manufacturing projects that reduce product cycle time and increase product quality. Knowledge includes:
- Finite element developer
- Unigraphics, CAD packages including CATIA and Autocad
- Ability to write integration software in C, C++, FORTRAN, Pascal or Basic
- Multiple platforms including Cray, Stardent, HP/Apollo, SGI, Sun

EXPERIENCE

Mastermind Engineering, Indianapolis, Indiana   1992-Present
Technical engineering firm specializing in aircraft, spacecraft and missile engine components.

Engineering Consultant   1995-Present
- Led team of ten software developers in projects including functional specification, cost and time estimating and prototype development.
- Managed development and implementation of in-house computer training of technical staff.
- Oversaw development of innovative integrated system for design and manufacture of compressor and turbine airfoils; system dramatically reduced design cycle time.

Engineer, Computer Utilization   1992-1995
- Introduced desktop computing that enhanced engineering productivity and user independence.

EDUCATION

B.S. Mechanical Engineering, Indiana University 1992
Continuing education includes courses in Ansys, Mastran, Unigraphics, Unix and Interleaf . . . Leadership in Technology . . . Teaching Computers . . . Communication Skills for Techies

MEMBERSHIPS AND RECOGNITION

National Association of Computer Trainers
Indiana Chapter of Engineers
First Place, Computer Science Award Mastermind Techie Project

HUMAN RESOURCES

OLIVE OIL
9998 Popeye Place
Chicago, Illinois 60601
(312) 944-2222

PROFILE

Human Resources manager with 15 years in organization development, high performance team building, staffing and training, labor relations, salary administration and compensation and benefits.

Superior leadership skills, extensive experience with TQM, executive management development and training. Known for ability to enhance profitability and support business objectives.

EXPERIENCE

Director, Human Resources   1994-Present
Liggett Manufacturing, Chicago, Illinois
Established new human resource department for flag manufacturer with 1,500 employees. Wrote policies for tenure, exempt and nonexempt status. Designed and implemented flexible benefits system.
Accomplishments:
- Initiated safety program that reduced accidents 60% within six months.
- Created new hiring standards that incorporated drug testing, reducing turnover 50% first year.
- Changed health care program to PPO, resulting in 30% savings.
- Launched pay for performance program, employee newsletter and communications program that dramatically increased employee morale.
- Developed and implemented written Affirmative Action Program.
- Trained self-directed work teams that increased productivity 75%.
- Developed Executive Team program that helped senior management create personal development plan.

Director, Human Resources   1990-1994
Cheney Donovan Homebuilders, Atlanta, Georgia
Created human resource department for southern homebuilding division using TQM techniques. Oversaw staffing of new director level positions, reengineering and organizational development and training.
Accomplishments:
- Researched theft problem that resulted in discharges without lawsuits.
- Implemented quality teams that resulted in process improvement at plants.
- Implemented salaried and hourly pay ranges.
- Incorporated exempt compensation program and salary administration to ensure guideline compliance.
- Initiated annual skills inventory and performance reviews.
- Instituted Effective Leadership Course for executives and management.

Olive Oil, page 2

Manager, Human Resources and Employee Relations   1982-1989
<u>Uhlmann Manufacturing</u>, Atlanta, Georgia
Oversaw staffing, personnel development, compensation and union relations for division
that manufactures machine tool equipment.
> <u>Accomplishments:</u>
> • Resolved downsizing and discharge cases with no lawsuits.
> • Developed and presented compensation training for middle management.
> • Initiated "Chats with Chet" communication program between employees and company president.
> • Successfully negotiated five-year labor agreements with union.
> • Instituted safety and security programs.

EDUCATION

B.S., Management, Atlanta State University 1982
Sanger Center for Leadership
Employee Relations Center for Continuing Education

PROFESSIONAL AFFILIATIONS

Greater Atlanta Human Resource Professionals
International Society of Human Resource Managers

INFORMATION SYSTEMS

CLARK LABEL
8900 Bucket Way
Washington, DC 20006
(202) 637-0000

SUMMARY

Progressive information systems professional with experience managing information systems and computer processing. Proven abilities to direct and troubleshoot software development, design digital computer systems, analyze networks and teach programmer skills, computer theory and software applications.

Goal-oriented and committed to cost-effective business solutions. Specific knowledge encompasses:
- Assembly language and high-level language interface
- Unix, C, Pascal, Assembly languages
- Systems integration
- Foreign video and electrical requirements
- Video subsystems
- Real-time software control and device drivers
- Multiuser systems development and supervision
- Distributed system applications

EXPERIENCE

Director, Manager Information Systems   1993-1997
Largo Computer, Inc., Washington, DC
Evaluate and recommend systems and networks for $30 million computer manufacturer. Teach network installation, operating systems, microcomputer manufacturing to technical teams. Supervise 20 staff members. Manage information systems, installations and production.
- Troubleshot and repaired over fifty types of computer hardware on site allowing businesses to continue operation with minimal interruption.
- Supervised team of network installers responsible for incorporating computer networking into business that gave companies OSI standard communication and internetworking.

Fulbright Fellow with Columbia University   1990-1992
Conducted ethnomusicological research using microcomputers

EDUCATION

M.B.A. Wharton School 1990
M.S. Mathematics Cornell University 1987
B.S. Mathematics Columbia University 1984

LAW

FELIPPE MORTIMAR
54 Edith Road, N.W.
Oklahoma City, Oklahoma 73110
(405) 840-2222

SUMMARY

Team-oriented professional with 17 years' extensive experience in chemical and light mechanical patent practice with a reputation for preparing and prosecuting difficult patent cases.

Proven strengths to:
- Counsel technical and management staff
- Give persuasive presentations
- Analyze patents, chemical inventions, new products and processes
- Write legal documents
- Research prior art

Successful track record in:
- Litigation support
- Patentability and novel searches
- Patent applications
- Evaluations and infringement opinions
- Prosecution
- Secrecy agreements
- Licensing agreements
- Research & Development
- Patent legislation
- Consumer product protection and processes
- Knowledge of legislative and regulatory processes

EXPERIENCE

<u>Woester & Francis</u>, Fortune 500 consumer products manufacturer, Patent Division
Oklahoma City, Oklahoma   1986-Present
Senior Patent Attorney
Counsel technical, legal and management staff, negotiate and draft legal documents and prosecute patents for producer consumer industrial product research, development and manufacturing. Draft and coordinate foreign patents.
- Obtained patents in over 90% of all cases filed.
- Received early patent allowances in a majority of patent cases within two years of filing.
- Presented papers to National Bar Association and National Patent Law Association.
- Trained new patent attorneys on how to successfully work with U.S. Patent Examining Corporation.

Felippe Mortimar, page 2

Swinedipp, Tipp and Lucent, Attorneys-at-Law, Patent Counsel for Xerox   1976-1986
Stamford, Connecticut
Attorney
Organized patent cases for filing overseas and in the U.S. Patent and Trademark Office.
Patent preparation, prosecution and litigation support.

Dulont, Chemical Division   1973-1975
Allentown, Pennsylvania
Research Chemist
Researched and developed new polymer coating and resin for large manufacturer of heavy chemicals, glass and paints.

EDUCATION

Juris Doctor, Capital University Law School 1973
B.S. Chemistry, Ohio State University 1968

Continuing Education in all areas of intellectual property law including litigation, reissue, reexamination, patent preparation, prosecution and patent appeals and trademark and copyright case law.

BAR ADMISSIONS

State of Oklahoma, State of Connecticut, State of Pennsylvania, U.S. Patent and Trademark Office and U.S. Court of Appeals for the Federal Circuit, U.S. Supreme Court

MEMBERSHIPS

American Bar Association
National Patent Law Association and Oklahoma City Intellectual Property Law Association, board member

MARKET RESEARCH (ADMINISTRATION)

MAX PARESH
21 Artsy Drive
Wichita, Kansas 67219
(316) 832-2222

PROFESSIONAL SUMMARY

An innovative problem solver with 15 years in market research and key decision-making roles that led to increased productivity. Known for ability to assess situations, strategies and interpersonal dynamics with objectivity and reason.

Reputation for leading others to meet common goals and objectives while enhancing personal contribution and overall productivity.

Knowledge encompasses:
- Business operations and management
- Project management
- Training
- Client relations
- Sales and marketing presentations
- Personnel functions
- Consumer package goods and services
- Qualitative and quantitative research
- Research techniques
- Marketing, promotion and advertising
- Consumer and societal trends

ACCOMPLISHMENTS

- Instrumental in establishing new market research business that has grown 40% annually into a $10 million customer-driven company within six years.

- Designed, implemented and analyzed study for fast-food chain on which company based its new marketing strategy, resulting in turnaround of five-year sales decline.

- Developed and gave presentation at conference on state-of-the-art research equipment that landed new $1 million client.

- Wrote proposal that persuaded management to implement four-day work week; gave staff more flexibility, met company objectives and increased productivity by 30%.

- Trained technical and professional staff on new research service within six months that resulted in $2 million of new business annually.

- Designed company profit-sharing system that distributes profits proportionate to individual's contribution; employees cite program as key morale booster.

EXPERIENCE

<u>Benning & Associates Research</u>, Wichita, Kansas   1990-Present
Vice President
Manage accounts for full-service, custom marketing research firm serving 45 national clients including packaged goods, consumer and financial services, restaurants, health care and telecommunications.
- Give sales presentations, oversee client relations, design research studies and analyze and present results.
- Lead team of 38 staff members in development and execution of research studies.
- Develop and monitor company mission and strategy.

<u>Bickel Research</u>, Columbus, Ohio   1982-1989
Regional Director   1987-1989
Marketed research services for $30 million market research firm via sales presentations and industry conference speeches. Analyzed and presented research study results. Developed new research technology.

Senior Executive   1985-1987
Developed research techniques including testing of television, print and billboard advertising. Managed six technical support staff members. Oversaw hiring and training.

Account Executive   1983-1985
Handled $700 thousand in client accounts. Presented research study findings.

Project Director   1982
Managed marketing research studies.

EDUCATION

M.B.A. in Marketing   Kansas State University   1992
B.S. in Marketing   Ohio State University   1982
Total Quality Leadership Training . . . Value Selling Workshop

MEMBERSHIPS

American Marketing Association

COMMUNITY

Division Chairperson, Fine Arts Fund 1994, 1995
Board of Directors, Big Brothers Association 1990-1997
Call to Art Fundraising Chair, 1993

ROSS VAN COUPLING
5922 Littlestone Way
Homer, Arkansas 99602
(907) 236-2222

SUMMARY

A creative leader with a wealth of experience in community, nonprofit and multicultural settings. Known for ability to build effective teams and inspire individuals to meet goals and objectives.

Proven strengths to:
- Work well with diverse groups
- Envision and develop strategic solutions to organizational problems
- Research and analyze complex situations, strategies and relationships

Knowledge encompasses:
- Sound management principles including team building, training, supervision, conflict management, financial management, program development
- Working with volunteers, boards and government groups
- Fund-raising, grant writing and administration
- Cultural adjustment processes
- Legislation related to human rights
- Research and documentation
- French and Spanish

ACHIEVEMENTS

- Led development of first Peace Among People two-day conference that involved Hindu, Muslim, Unitarian, Catholic, Jewish, Siek and Native American communities resulting in honest dialogue and understanding of differences and cultural history.

- Researched and documented effects of nuclear waste program that supported linkage between disease and local industry.

- Analyzed organizational structure of regional nonprofit agency and created personnel policies with a cooperative management philosophy that dramatically enhanced morale and increased productivity.

- Analyzed root causes of conflict within national nonprofit organization and proposed solutions that reduced conflict and helped numerous multicultural groups reach common ground.

EXPERIENCE

Director   1995-1997
Peace International, Atlanta, Georgia
Founded and oversaw operation of national organization that promotes dialogue between
races and cultures in U.S. Recruited 300 volunteers, established Board of Directors, developed operating procedures and training programs. Researched and implemented process
to obtain government funding. Initiated and oversaw special projects and events.

Assistant Director   1990-1995
Cleveland Fair Housing Association, Cleveland, Ohio
Assisted with daily operations of nonprofit agency that acted as watchdog for enforcement
of fairhousing laws. Developed brochures on Cleveland communities that marketed area
to new residents. Coordinated Community Housing Resource Board, including members
from Chamber of Commerce, real estate, banking and local community groups.

Staff Assistant   1986-1990
Refugee Aid International, Washington, DC
Administered programs for nonprofit agency that assists refugees in need. Developed and
wrote human rights/refugee newsletter. Member of task force that worked closely with
South American countries. Developed training for volunteers. Conducted extensive research on cultural adjustment processes and human rights conditions. Wrote grants and
supervised two interns.

Instructor   1981-1983
George Washington Community College, Arlington, Virginia
Taught undergraduate courses in Anthropology and Sociology. Conducted in-depth re-
search for Ethnic Studies Program.

EDUCATION

B.A. in Anthropology/Sociology   George Washington University   1980
M.A. in Cultural Anthropology and International Administration   Union Institute   1984

Continuing education includes Volunteer Management

NURSING

ELEANOR ROSSVELT
23 East Fine Way
Antioch, Tennessee 37012
(615) 731-2222

SUMMARY OF QUALIFICATIONS

Health care professional committed to quality care while containing costs. Extensive clinical, training and administrative background as nurse educator, recruiter and staff nurse. Background encompasses utilization review with proven strengths to organize and coordinate programs, supervise, train and effectively work with medical and administrative staff.

<u>**Education includes**</u>:

Associate Degree in Applied Science-Nursing, University of Tennessee 1976
Tennessee Board of Nursing License LPN
Illinois Board of Nursing License LPN

EXPERIENCE

Training

<u>Antioch Hospital</u>, Antioch, Tennessee   1993-1997
Nurse In-service Educator

Developed and presented in-service classes on new trends in patient care. Updated policies and procedures.

- Tracked staff compliance of state and facility in-service requirements.
- Trained staff on use of new equipment.
- Organized and presented new employee orientation.

Administrative

<u>Price Costello Review Group</u>, Chicago, Illinois   1988-1993
Review Administrator

Reviewed medical records for hospitals in Chicago area to assess quality of care and utilization. Developed review procedures.

Recruitment

<u>Chicago Hope</u>, Chicago, Illinois   1984-1987
Nurse Recruiter

Developed network with nursing students and instructors at area colleges and schools of nursing for general acute care hospital. Worked closely with nurse managers to determine staffing needs.

- Coordinated interviews with nurse managers and job candidates.
- Assisted in development of nurse recruitment brochure.
- Coordinated college career days and health fairs.
- Acted as resource for staff on benefits, scholarships and tuition assistance programs.

Eleanor Rossvelt, page 2

Clinical

Chicago Hope, Chicago, Illinois   1978-1984

Charge Nurse/Staff Nurse, Medical Surgical Unit

Supervised nursing staff. Gave primary care. Worked closely with physicians to determine comprehensive plan of care.

• Member of Resident Care Planning Committee that developed care plan for patients including discharge planning, occupational therapy, physical therapy, dietary, social services and pharmacy requirements.

SALES/SALES MANAGEMENT

LOREN GREENOSKI
111 Piedmont Ponderosa
Dallas, Texas 75201
(214) 740-2222

OBJECTIVE

Sales or sales management position that will contribute to the development of long-term client relationships and produce profitable sales growth.

SUMMARY OF QUALIFICATIONS

Seven-year track record of successful sales experience with strengths to plan, persuade, follow through and develop trusting relationships. Expertise includes:
- New business development
- Sales proposals
- Planning and budgets
- Contract negotiations

EXPERIENCE

Travolta Associates, Dallas, Texas   1990-1997
District Sales Manager   1993-1997
Oversaw new business development and account management for three-state area for second largest asset valuation firm in U.S. Initiated business plan for district and converted sales administration from manual to computerized system.
   ACHIEVEMENTS:
   - Increased sales 50% in first year during recessionary economy.
   - Gained access to decision makers in Fortune 100 firms, municipalities, hospitals and universities that resulted in higher market penetration.
   - Saved account worth $2.5 million with Fortune 500 company by negotiating agreement with senior managers.

Account Executive   1990-1993
Conducted cold calls that led to consulting relationships with attorneys and CPA firms. Gave sales presentations and serviced up to 120 accounts.
   ACHIEVEMENTS:
   - Increased business by 50% within first six months on the job.
   - Named top producing sales professional two consecutive years.

EDUCATION

B.A. Marketing Texas State University 1990
Seminars include: The Art of Closing the Sale, New Leadership, Negotiating to Win

SALES AND MARKETING

KYLE LANE
9009 Brezhnev Avenue
Santa Monica, California 90406
(310) 399-2222

PROFILE

Results-oriented sales and marketing manager with diversified experience in consumer package goods. Experience includes long-range business plans and forecasting. Skilled in managing and motivating teams and coordinating marketing programs to enhance customer relations.

EXPERIENCE

Haley Beauty Care Company, Los Angeles, California   1990-1997
Manager, Sales & Merchandising   1994-1997
Developed sales strategies, promotion and merchandising plans for $9 billion division of Fortune 500 consumer products manufacturer.
- Awarded Gold Club Membership for outstanding sales and leadership.
- Overhauled distribution system that significantly reduced inventory and improved customer service.
- Oversaw transition of business acquisition from East to West coast with little business disruption.
- Developed and implemented new system to more efficiently manage forecasting and production planning.
- Managed acquisition and divestiture of three divisions.

Manager, Sales & Marketing Services   1990-1993
Managed 65-member department that handles sales planning, promotion and administration of $6 billion division.
- Initiated bracket pricing that saved company $750 million in one year.
- Developed new procedures that significantly reduced customer order/cycle time.
- Implemented broker sales network that exclusively handled beauty care products and significantly enhanced relationships with customers.

EDUCATION

M.B.A. University of California at Los Angeles 1994
B.S. in Business Administration Pepperdine University 1989
Computer knowledge: Word for Windows, Excel, PowerPoint

Seminars include: Total Quality, Team Building, Promotion, Merchandising and Advertising, Management for Marketers

New Graduate Resumes

NEW GRAD

WANDA WIND
5689 West Whipple Way
Atlanta, Georgia 30364
(404) 238-2221

OBJECTIVE

Position that utilizes skills to:
- Plan educational activities and programs
- Clearly communicate ideas and concepts
- Facilitate mutual understanding between diverse groups of people
- Conceptualize and implement projects from beginning to end
- Advocate significant issues
- Apply creative problem-solving approaches to interpersonal and organizational issues

SUMMARY OF QUALIFICATIONS

- B.A. Communication, Minor in Women's Studies New York University 1997
- Mature and articulate communicator and thorough planner

Four years' educational and hands-on experience working one-on-one with economically and culturally diverse people, including international cultures in nonprofit and business settings. Known for ability to support and motivate others and inspire teamwork to meet goals and objectives. Specific areas of knowledge and experience include:

- Workshop development and presentation
- Training
- Volunteer recruitment
- Working with task forces and nonprofit organizations
- Women's issues
- Working with Spanish and French cultures
- Fluency in French
- Issues related to low-income citizens and people with mental and physical disabilities

- Fund-raising
- Market research
- Special event planning

EXPERIENCE

Nonprofit:

Intern, Loffing Center   1996
Atlanta, Georgia
Created and implemented programs that helped homeless women locate employment and housing. Conducted interviews, led resident meetings. Planned and coordinated trips for staff to tour shelters, jails and rehab housing.
- Organized and presented workshops on diversity and job interview process that led to building of women's self-esteem and ability to be productive citizens.
- Tutored residents to prepare for GED, giving them educational credentials to obtain employment.
- Oversaw donation program that resulted in 50% increase in local corporate gifts.

Intern, Yinning Rollands Home   Summer 1995
Atlanta, Georgia
Acted as liaison between clients and agency that provides information on food and clothing for the needy. Member of problem-solving task force. Promoted agency at volunteer and job fairs. Assisted with coordination of annual fund-raiser. Coordinated volunteers.
  • Initiated recruitment of volunteers that significantly increased awareness of organization and volunteer base.

Intern, Independent Living for Cerebral Palsy   Summer 1993
Atlanta, Georgia
Assisted residents with daily tasks and dealing with emotional aspects of being physically challenged. Led small group therapy sessions.
  • Acted as liaison between residents and Director of Cerebal Palsy Foundation to rectify funding allowance.

Volunteer, Amnesty International   Summer 1992
New York, New York
Assisted in coordination and implementation of letter-writing campaign and fund-raiser that led to eventual release of Turkish political prisoners.

International:

Au Pair for French Family   1997
Paris, France
Oversaw daily activities and care of two-year-old child and running of family household. Organized social outings with neighborhood families. Researched and implemented nutritionally balanced diet for family. Created educational activities and outings. Taught English to child.

Market Researcher, Yankee Shirts   1994
Paris, France
Conducted market research for American retail manufacturer that resulted in entry into international market.

Business:

Intern/Tutor, Rojanka Inez Foundation   Winter 1995
Atlanta, Georgia
Oversaw tutoring service for Hispanic workers and families relocated to area. Designed and presented curriculum on English language. Organized educational field trips, activities and entertainment that aided cultural assimilation.

NEW GRAD

RANADA RAINTREE
New Vintage Lane
Beverly Hills, California 90212
(213) 655-2222

OBJECTIVE

To contribute to the overall efficiency and smooth operations of a health care organization in a position of significant responsibility that utilizes proven abilities to:
- Plan, organize and coordinate schedules, procedures and systems
- Initiate and follow through on details of complex projects
- Train others to ensure thorough understanding of internal processes
- Solve operational problems
- Work well with management, staff and elderly clientele

QUALIFICATIONS

A goal-oriented professional with hands-on and educational experience in health services administration in U.S. and Europe. Known for ability to build consensus among management and staff and conduct research that leads to informed decisions. Great empathy and appreciation for mature adults.

- Masters in Health Services Administration with concentration in long-term care California State College at Fullerton, 1997, G.P.A. 3.78
- Bachelor of Art in Psychology, University of Notre Dame, 1994, G.P.A. 3.09, Dean's List 1994, 1993
- Coursework and experience includes exposure to: Total Quality Management, Strategic Management and Planning, Accounting, Finance, Budgeting and Statistical Analysis, Teams
- Solid understanding of adult development, psychological aging and ethics related to elderly
- Familiar with community-based services
- Proficient in computers

ACHIEVEMENTS

- Assisted in implementation of new computer inventory system for 65-bed skilled nursing facility that cut time to order, track and bill for medical supplies from one week to one day per month.
- Spearheaded maintenance and repair of health care facility for inspection by new owners that resulted in approval and passage of fire and safety codes and biannual inspections.
- Trained administrative and nursing staff on value of generating and tracking valid statistical data in spreadsheet format that resulted in more accurate quality assurance tools to determine residents' health.
- Coordinated and analyzed data to determine feasibility of price increase in assisted living unit; produced a uniform system for tracking rental rates that gave management tool to consistently measure revenue.

Ranada Raintree, page 2

- Received excellent ratings from management, residents and staff as nurse aide and team member in an 85-bed nursing facility in foreign country.
- Led coordination of resident activities through interaction with management and staff that resulted in smooth running operation of up to 12 daily programs.
- Researched and initiated implementation of standing ethics committee that standardized policies and alleviated stressful decision making during medical crises.
- Developed spreadsheet that clearly illustrated annual spending trends and cost allocations.

EXPERIENCE

Administrative Resident   1997
Brookwood Retirement Community, Los Angeles, California
Assisted administrator in daily operations of 65-bed skilled nursing unit and 75-apartment assisted living wing. Analyzed and computerized internal forms to monitor facility's financial status and resident care. Researched and reported to management on internal operations.

Nurse Assistant   1995-1996
Ludingham Home for the Elderly, London, England
Assisted with daily care and transporting of residents.

ACTIVITIES

- Attended semester in Hamburg, Germany, through Student International Program
- Club, varsity and competitive runner: Chicago Marathon, 10-K marathons
- California State College and University of Notre Dame Alumni Clubs
- American College of Health Care Administrators
- Southern Valley Gerontology Council
- Student Chapter California Association of Adult Daycare

LAURA LUMINA
669 Rickety Lane
Brookfield, Connecticut 06804
(203) 775-2222

OBJECTIVE

Position in Interior Design and Architectural firm that utilizes theoretical knowledge and hands-on experience in design.

QUALIFICATIONS

- B.S. in Interior Design
  Siena College of Art and Design, Loudonville, New York 1997

- Interior Design & Architecture Seminar, School of the Art Institute of Chicago 1996

- Awarded Best Design, Motorola Design Competition 1996
- Strengths:
  - Conscientious, quick learner with passion for design and architecture
  - Conceptualize and determine functional and spatial requirements
  - Play layout of architectural projects
  - Prepare scale and full-size drawings
  - Utilize CADD programs to develop floor plans, elevations and perspective drawings

- Coursework and experience in:
  - Schematic and bubble diagrams, signage and logo design
  - Fabric and finish selection
  - Reflected ceiling plans
  - Space planning
  - Section and elevation drawings
  - Lighting schedules
  - Architectural design styles

EXPERIENCE

Phillips Architectural Environments, Brookfield, Connecticut   Winter 1996
Intern
Worked closely with sales representatives to develop quotes and confirm order schedules for national architectural firm specializing in office environments. Utilized CADD to draft open floor plan. Updated resource library, showroom prices and new accessory lines. Assisted in furniture and fabric selection. Compiled sample bid binders.

Laura Lumina, page 2

Casepoint Design, New York, New York   Summer 1995
<u>Design Assistant/Intern</u>
Assisted in planning of 30,000 square feet of military base office space for commercial design firm. Measured floor space and selected office furniture. Updated library with current product line and fabric samples.

Lucent Design, Boston, Massachusetts   Summer 1994
<u>Design Assistant/Intern</u>
Assisted commercial design firm with projects that included selection and assembly of sample board for office in Metropolitan Museum of Art. Updated floor plans for office. Accompanied designers to assess client needs.

ACTIVITIES

Student Association of Illuminating Engineers
Association of Business Designers

NEW GRAD

LLOYD LIVETT
5521 Cyber Spaceway, Ephraim, Utah 84627 • (512) 238-2222

SUMMARY OF QUALIFICATIONS
Responsible, determined and self-motivated professional with the ability to analyze and evaluate complex legal cases, strategies and statutory doctrine, express ideas succinctly and summarize with clarity and insight.
- Broad academic experience and solid grounding in classic liberal arts
- Comprehensive knowledge of corporate tax law with exposure to international, estate and gift taxation, income taxation of trusts and estates and taxation of compensation
- Member of Utah Bar

EDUCATION

Master of Law in Taxation 1997
University of Pennsylvania School of Law
GPA 3.8

Juris Doctor 1995
Capital University School of Law
Ranked in top 15% of class
Tax GPA 3.5

Bachelor of Arts 1990
Seton Hill College
Major in History
Language Study Abroad, London, England

EXPERIENCE

<u>Research Assistant</u>, Capital University, School Law
Columbus, Ohio   1993
Conducted research and drafted text for casebook entitled International Law.

<u>Judicial Extern</u>, Honorable Joan Van Buren, Northern District Court of Utah
Salt Lake City, Utah   Summer 1992
Researched and analyzed motions. Researched and prepared bench memoranda for Ninth Circuit cases.

<u>Research Assistant</u>, Legal Aid Society of Ephraim
Ephraim, Utah   1991
Conducted legal research on civil rights and consumer protection issues.

Lloyd Livett, page 2

Congressional Intern, Congresswoman Patricia Greer
Washington, DC   Fall 1990
Handled correspondence and telephone calls from constituents, oversaw mailing of quarterly newsletter.

ACCOMPLISHMENTS

• Received Institute of American Tax Award for Excellence in Taxation.

• Received highest grade in International Tax Planning and Tax and Estate Planning for Closely Held Interests courses.

• As part of class in intellectual property, researched and wrote on patentability requirement of nonobviousness of invention, one of the vaguest central doctrines of patent law.

NEW GRAD

RANDALL REMAR
56 Shantel Road
Toronto, Ontario M4N 2L6 Canada
(416) 781-2222

OBJECTIVE

A position that contributes to the education and welfare of others by using abilities to teach concepts and ideas, guide individuals to achieve goals and objectives and work well in a team environment.

QUALIFICATIONS

- A responsible professional with a passion for helping others.
- Known for warm personality, sense of humor and ability to see situations objectively.
- Hands-on and educational experience includes broad exposure to business operations and sciences and their effect on daily life.
- Strong interest in the environment and conservation.

EDUCATION

B.S. Science, Minor in Psychology DePauw University, 1997, Magna Cum Laude
Working towards completion of Teaching Certificate
Currently studying Sign Language

ACHIEVEMENTS

- Counseled junior high school students on interpersonal relationships and family issues that greatly enhanced their self-esteem and personal confidence.

- Assisted camp naturalist in workshop presentations on wildlife and surviving in the wilderness.

- Assisted biology instructor in presenting theories and conducting lab tests that helped students gain in-depth understanding of living organisms and vital processes.

- Led over 100 students in establishment and implementation of goals and objectives for nonprofit social organization involved in dozens of community service projects.

- Instrumental in creating ways to motivate students to volunteer for event that raised $3,000 for Juvenile Diabetes.

- Initiated and succeeded in campaign to get cellular telephone company to donate 500 phones to neighborhood crime watch programs.

Randall Remar, page 2

EXPERIENCE

<u>College employment:</u>   1986-1992
Bookseller, Read & Feed Bookstore . . . **Child Care Provider**, Tabian Day Care.

ACTIVITIES AND AWARDS

- National Honor Society . . . Golden Key Honor Society . . . Omega Summa Award . . .
  Alpha Sigma Fraternity President
- Volunteer, Toronto Zoo and Botanical Garden

NEW GRAD

LANA TARNER
8900 Zippie Lane
Ashburn, Virginia 22012
(703) 723-2222

OBJECTIVE

Customer Service position that contributes to the efficiency and effectiveness of an organization and utilizes strengths to anticipate and follow through on customer needs and communicate with enthusiasm and clarity.

QUALIFICATIONS

Bright, dedicated team player who is comfortable dealing with the public. Hands-on experience in hospitality industry and customer service. Reputation as a quick learner and eager to exceed an organization's objectives.
- Associates Degree in Business, Wellington State University 1997
- In-depth knowledge of computer hardware and software including DOS, Lotus, Basic, Windows, WordPerfect and Microsoft Works

EXPERIENCE

In college:

Hampster Inns of America, Miami, Florida   1996-1997
Customer Service Representative
Handled reservations and inquiries from hotel guests for new hotel property.
- Trained personnel on daily procedures that significantly contributed to smooth flow of operations.

Apple Cruise Line, Miami, Florida   Summer, 1995
Passenger Services Coordinator/Intern
Coordinated guest services activities of cruise ship. Resolved complaints from passengers. Confirmed airline flights and assisted with other services requested by passengers.
- Researched incidents of lost luggage and pets that resulted in resolution of problems and happy customers.

Community:

March of Dimes, Ashburn, Virginia   Summer, 1994
Volunteer Coordinator
- Recruited and coordinated volunteers to participate in March of Dimes event that contributed to exceeding of fundraising goals.

NEW GRAD

GLORIA VANDERLUST
23 East Flaverman
Pennington, New Jersey 08533
(609) 737-2222

OBJECTIVE

Position that builds on strong interest in finance, investments and economic theory and utilizes abilities to research and analyze information and communicate financial concepts.

Areas of interest: Securities analysis, portfolio management, cash management, trust account management.

QUALIFICATIONS

Career-oriented team player with broad exposure to business operations and hands-on experience in financial markets.
- B.S.B.A., Glouster University 1996
- 100% of education self-financed through financial investments
- Strong aptitude in math with coursework in business calculus, algebra, trigonometry
- Well versed in various investment approaches
- Active in investment club
- Avid reader of *The Wall Street Journal, Business Week, The New York Times* and other business and financial periodicals
- Senior projects include lease pricing analysis, LBO, mergers and acquisitions project

EXPERIENCE

Rothbart and Bartroth, Pennington, New Jersey   1997
Intern
Used telephone communication skills to generate leads for financial brokerage firm. Explained benefits of company's seminar to retirees. Gained understanding of how financial products are marketed.

Sawyer Palm Savings, Miami, Florida   1996
Intern/Loan Representative
Assisted with selling of mortgage products to real estate agents.

ACTIVITIES

Founder of Student Investment Club
Member, Student Chapter Financial Professionals of America

Yechy
Resumes

They are yechy for some of the reasons I talked about in "Bleahy Writing" in chapter five. Some use complete sentences. One has an objective that emphasizes security and promotions—the last reason the employer is motivated to talk to you, let alone hire you. Some just list a bunch of boring facts. They all lack pizzazz. And they look pretty bad.

When you read them, you don't get a feel for the people. And overall, you don't get answers to the four questions on the reader's mind:

1. What can you do?

2. Have you done it and stuck with it?

3. What do you know?

4. What kind of person are you?

Ronald McDonald

1415 Leroy Way
Hewitt, Texas 76643
(817) 666-2222

OBJECTIVE

To secure a position in the accounting environment

EDUCATION
1995-1998

Hewitt Community College
Hewitt, Texas
Associate degree in Accounting
Estimated Graduation date: May 1998

1986-1988

Lower Valley JVS
Hewitt, Texas
Accounting
High School Graduate

SPECIAL SKILLS

- Lotus 1-2-3
- WordPerfect 5.1
- dBase 3
- Data Entry
- Related aspects of computerized & manual accounting including governmental and financial accounting

ACCOUNTING WORK EXPERIENCE
1986-1989

Watson Associates
Accountant (student)
Hewitt, Texas
Responsibilities included:
- Maintained all financial reports for company
- Handled accounts receivable
- Handled accounts payable
- Handled payments of all bills
- Deposited all cash receipts

ACHIEVEMENTS

- Lower Valley JVS Accounting Advisory Committee (1995)
- Outstanding Senior Accounting Professionals of America (1995)
- Outstanding Senior (1995)

REFERENCES UPON REQUEST

GRANT TROY
1100 Spellbound Ln.
Reno, Nevada 89519
(702) 786-2222

EDUCATION: graduated in June of 1997 from the University of Nevada with a bachelor of arts degree in advertising including fields of concentration in Psychology and English.

ADVERTISING WORK EXPERIENCE:
Freelance Copywriting Projects:
    Sena County Board of Education—Tech Prep Curriculum Committee
    -currently writing copy for brochures/direct mail/radio formats.

    Swift Fitness Center
    -wrote and designed newspaper advertisements.

OTHER WORK EXPERIENCE:
Little Old Food Joint, January 1996-Present
position: server and busser manager.

Schuller's Wigwam, August 1993-August 1995
duties included delivery, taking food orders, clean up, etc.

AWARDS/HONORS:
received two ADDY Awards for creative excellence in February of 1995 in the following categories: student corporate identity and logo; and student direct mail piece.

received three ADDY Awards for creative excellence in February of 1994 in the following categories: student print ad, student print campaign, and student radio ad.

ADVERTISING RELATED ACTIVITIES:
member of Reno Ad Club, member of University of Nevada American Advertising Federation, served as AAF professional development chairperson, have volunteered with the Ad Club, have twice attended the National Advertising Conference's copywriting workshops.

ADVERTISING RELATED SKILLS:
proficient in Microsoft Word and WordPerfect, currently learning Quark XPress.

capable of illustrating, examples included in portfolio.

PORTFOLIO AND REFERENCES AVAILABLE ON REQUEST.

FRANCES Segunda
4126 Maxine Drive
Scottsdale, Arizona 85252
(602) 945-2222

JOB
OBJECTIVE: To secure a upwardly mobile position with a progressive company where my Information Technology and other varied office skills would be of most benefit to an employer.

EXPERIENCE:

1994-Present: Scottsdale Energy, Scottsdale, Arizona
As a member of the Security Administration team, I was responsible for creating and maintaining a file of user logon ids including monitoring the mainframe accesses granted to each user on a Novell 3.1 network.

1993-1994:   Computer Programming Technology held at Augusta Industries, Phoenix, Arizona
As a graduate of this training program, I set up and maintained a Novell NetWare 2.2 network. In addition, I occasionally assisted the instructor by working one-on-one with the current students.

1992:   Riley & Associates, Phoenix, Arizona
I implemented a system to track hardware and software inventories on personal computers connected to a Local Area Network via Banyan Vines. I also upgraded the menuing system which was in use at that time.

1979-1984:   Jerome & Rice Associates, Phoenix, Arizona
As a Programmer/Analyst, I developed, implemented, and fully documented several major computer applications using, among other packages, DMSII data base on a Burroughs mainframe. I also developed several data entry applications used to capture input to these and other applications.

Hardware: Various mainframe and personal computers utilizing several versions of Novell NetWare, IBM LanManager 1.3, and Banyan Vines.

Software: Windows, COBOL, MicroSoft Access, Visual Basic, Word 6.0, MS-DOS 6.2, MVS JCL, TSO, ROSCOE, MEMO, and ACF2..

EDUCATION:
1995:   Loma Linda University
Bachelor of Science degree in Information Technology

VICTORIA VULCAN
454 Volking Ave.
Bowdoinham, Maine 04008
Home: (207) 665-2222
Office: (207) 665-1111

PROFESSIONAL EXPERIENCE (1990-Present)

• Negotiate for and advise business entities, financial institutions, and individuals in business and real estate transactions, including assistance in obtaining financing for start-up businesses.

• Consult with clients, and draft contracts, loan documents, leases, assignments, and other types of business documentation.

• Provide representation and advice to financial institutions regarding loan defaults, mortgage foreclosures, bankruptcy proceedings, and other collection matters.

• Draft documents and act as closing agent for real-estate financings of out-of-state company.

ACHIEVEMENTS (1978-1990)

• Provided advice and representation to financial institutions in daily banking matters, preparation of loan documentation, and negotiation of loans and loan workouts, foreclosures, collections, and bankruptcy.

• Represented local real estate developer in zoning, eminent domain proceedings, and complex litigation.

• Handled Chapter 11 bankruptcy for driving service company.

• Successfully represented and advised school building corporation board members as to all legal issues involved in the issuance of $10 million bond issue for construction of school.

• Advised park board on issues of funding, conflict, and liability.

• Organized and supervised Robb & Shipley's office staff.

Victoria Vulcan, page 2

EDUCATION

University of Maine   1978-1983
J.D.: May, 1983

University of Maine   1970-1974
B.A.: English, 1974 ("with Distinction")

BAR ADMISSIONS

Maine Bar (Admitted 1983)

The Colorado Bar (Admitted 1984)

PROFESSIONAL MEMBERSHIPS

Maine State Bar Association

American Bar Association

LEGAL EMPLOYMENT HISTORY

Attorney-Keeley, Kahn & Katz   1993-Present
Indianapolis, Indiana.

Attorney-Robb & Shipley   1990-1992
Donnerville, Massachusetts.

Partner-Bonney, Booie & Bowes   1987-1990
Donnerville, Massachusetts.

Attorney-Monson, Bronson & Johnson, of Counsel to Jensen, Benson, 1984-1987
Densen, Rapunzel & Neubauer
Wheaton, Illinois.

Solo Practice   1983-1984
Boston, Massachusetts

REFERENCES
Available upon request

Once You've Got Your Resume

YOU'RE BETTER PREPARED FOR INTERVIEW QUESTIONS

Well, why not? After developing the kind of resume I just covered, you'll know answers to:

- What are your strengths?
- Give me an example of how you've applied them.
- Tell me about something you did that you're most proud of.
- What did you do in your job at the Ying Yang Company?
- Why should I hire you?
- Why are you qualified for this position?
- Tell me about yourself.
- What do you know about (fill in the blank)?
- How do others describe you? or What kind of person are you?

With practice and preparation, you'll do one heck of a job in informational and job interviews.

YOU'RE CLOSER TO GETTING THE JOB YOU WANT

If you develop the type of resume I've covered here, you'll know a lot more about yourself by just going through the process. This increases your odds of getting the job you want because you can describe what you have to offer, you believe in it and you've got proof to show you can do it. You can package yourself in a way that helps others understand your value. Even if you're not absolutely sure what you're going after, you'll have a document that helps others help you figure it out.

WHEN YOU'RE READY TO USE IT

Get to know and believe every word of your resume. Be prepared to explain in more detail what you mean by a statement. Otherwise, when an interviewer asks you about something on your resume, you'll find yourself bluffing your way through an explanation.

Then use every tool out there in your job search. Recruiters, electronic job banks, newspaper ads and trade journals. But spend most of your time doing the following:

1. Talk to people you already know. Friends, family, neighbors, dentist, stockbroker, realtor, former co-workers and bosses. People whose opinions you trust. Tell them all about you. Don't assume they know. Most likely, they're familiar with one side of you—not the details of your professional life.

Describe your experience, skills you've honed, achievements you've scored. Tell them your career objective. Ask for ideas on how to achieve it. Ask about companies you're interested in targeting.

What's a company's reputation? Are they growing? Ask them if they know other people you can talk to to get similar advice. And don't forget to leave your resume.

2. Go meet with the people your friends and acquaintances referred you to. (Most people will be happy to meet when you tell them someone *they* know and like sent you.) Take your resume. Ask them similar questions. Brainstorm. People are full of information. And they know people who know other people who have ideas of where you can find what you're looking for. They may even know of jobs that are a perfect match.

3. Keep your positioning and thesis statements posted on your wall. This will help you stay focused during your search.

WHEN YOU GET AN OFFER

Don't accept it until you've really thought it through. Talk it over with someone who can be objective. Evaluate six things:

1. The actual position. Make sure you understand exactly what you'll be doing. Get a job description. Does it sound like something you'd enjoy? Will you be challenged?

2. The company. Will you feel good about working there? Does it have a good reputation? Are management's values similar to yours? Do you believe in the company's product or service?

3. The environment. Do you feel comfortable there? Is it a place where you will be productive?

4. The people. How do you feel about the person you'd report to? How about the staff you'd work with or that would work for you?

5. The salary. Will you be paid for the value you bring to the position? Is there potential to increase your salary? Are there incentives?

6. The benefits. How's the overall package?

ONCE YOU GET THE JOB YOU WANT

In your new job you'll be exposed to fresh ideas, you'll grow and get thoughts on where you want to head next. You may even get a notion for a new career. So while all this is going on:

1. Jot down new achievements, projects you're working on, classes you've taken and knowledge you've acquired. Keep this information in one place—a notebook or computer.

2. Update your resume with this information every three to six months.

3. Don't wait until you need a resume to rustle up a new one—like the day you hear about a position that you'd like to interview for or the day you're out of a job.

4. Regularly ask yourself: Am I doing what I want? Am I enjoying this? Am I using my strengths? Am I excited about getting up in the morning? Am I challenged? Is this helping me get to the next stage of my career? If not, don't wait to change your situation. Do something that day.

5. Update your career objective as you reach and set new goals. Write a new thesis statement. When you update your resume, make sure the qualifications and experience you list on the resume support your new objective.

6. Stay tuned into lifestyle trends, and keep tabs on where your industry is headed.

And finally, meet new people and keep old friends and associates posted of your whereabouts. People who know you and like you will help. So tell them about your dreams. Cause ya never know.

RESUME STRATEGIES AT A GLANCE

THREE THINGS TO POST ON YOUR WALL WHILE WRITING YOUR RESUME
The Goal of Your Resume:

To hook and hold someone's attention and show them how you can improve their life.

Your Positioning Statement:

What one, simple message do you want employers to get about you?

Your Thesis Statement:

What you want and can do for a company and how you'll make a difference.

TO WRITE A THESIS STATEMENT

Determine:

1. What you want to do
2. What you can do
3. How you will make a difference

EIGHT THINGS PEOPLE WASTE TIME WORRYING ABOUT

1. Who might read your resume and what they'll think
2. Whether you should write a resume for each job you apply for
3. Whether it should be one, two or three pages
4. How you're going to deal with that gap in your job history
5. How to deal with the fact that you have no experience
6. How to deal with the fact that you're over fifty
7. How to handle the fact that you were fired or quit your last job
8. That all your experience was in nonprofit organizations or education or with one company

THE KIND OF RESUME THAT WILL GET YOU THE JOB YOU WANT

It will:

1. Capture the most unique and interesting facts and characteristics about you that support your immediate career goal
2. Tell what skills and knowledge you have
3. Give an overview of your career—what you've done and where
4. Show how you've made things better in the past and what you have the potential of doing in the future
5. Use attention-grabbing, specific, action-oriented language
6. Invite someone to want to know more

WHO MAY WANT TO SEE YOUR RESUME

1. Recruiters
2. Human resource professionals
3. Other people in companies
4. Friends, family and other well-meaning folks

FOUR THINGS MOST EVERYONE WANTS TO KNOW ABOUT YOU

1. What can you do? (Abilities)
2. Have you done it and stuck with it? (Related experiences)
3. What do you know? (Knowledge)
4. What kind of person are you? (Personal attributes)

INDEX